THE INNER SOLAR SYSTEM

THE INNER
S☽LAR
SYSTEM

ISBN 978-1-7384218-0-0

THE INNER SOLAR SYSTEM

BEING AMAZING
THE NEW NORMAL

P J LOFTUS

For Carolyn

Foreword

Even if we have no knowledge or interest in astrology, if we look up at the night sky we cannot help but feel awestruck by the majesty of our natural world. Nature is the key here and just as it exists outside and all around us, so too does it exist inside of us. The belief that we humans are somehow separate from nature is one of the greatest wounding that mankind can experience. This belief has created division and destruction, not only of our beloved planet earth, but for each one of us individually. Can we bring unity to our world and our often beleaguered selves? This is the question that has perplexed the greatest of scientific and spiritual minds from Einstein to Jung and continues to challenge us as we evolve in consciousness.

Not all of us have an epiphany experience, as Pennie had on embarking on her journey of greater understanding of what it is to be fully human and fully divine. Most of us, however, have experienced moments of synchronicity; times when we felt "at one" with ourselves and with the world. In these moments we experience a sensation of being in flow, in the miracle zone, or in Pennie's words, "amazing". Pennie guides us to recognise that what we may once have deemed extraordinary is more accessible than we ever thought possible. Rather than slipping in and out of the miracle zone, we were created as miraculous beings born to be in flow. Miraculous beings in the very slipstream of love itself. The awesomeness of the universe exists within each one of us.

As Above, So Below.

Christina Masterman,

Soul Integration, Rediscovering the Sacred

Contents

Introduction

This book is a catalyst for remembering who you really are for your highest good. It has the intention to enable anyone to connect with their inner being and discover that there is, *in fact,* more to life.

If we are all honest with ourselves, we have asked the question, *'What's life all about? or 'Is this it?'*

At some point, we all decide to go in search of something more. For me, it was my *inner solar system* and I have come to believe that everybody can expand by doing the same.

Wouldn't it be nice to become empowered by having a tool you can use for yourself whenever you wish?

The great news is that this tool has no rules, and you can play with this information whenever you want.

This isn't solely metaphysical insight because science is catching up too.

We are moving from *just* chemistry to a mix of physics *and* chemistry which introduces the topic of *frequency*.

Frequency is what everything is made up of. It's the creative force behind all things and we all have our own personal frequencies.

Wouldn't you want to know your personal frequencies so you can co-create your best life?

By using your inner solar system and finding the personal frequency of your energy centres, you can release your pain from the root (if that is your journey) and clear your mental and emotional state so you can return to the centre of your inner solar system.

You can do this by knowing your *body map* and once you have this, you will know the specific frequencies for different parts of your body. Then, you can literally play that frequency (on your speakers, mobile phone or computer) and fill the room with this sound to evoke the frequency within, enabling your body, mind, and emotions to function more optimally.

Though this is a very powerful tool, it's just one part of a complex system that is you and throughout this book, we are going to explore your inner solar system in accessible detail.

I came across this work through my own personal story, through channeling, downloads, and consistently learning more about the information that I now *know* to be true (due to what I have experienced and been shown through my guides in my everyday life). Now, *we* wish to explain it straightforwardly to aid you in understanding some of the more complex workings that make up who you are.

This is a book that you can keep coming back to. It's not a one-time read. Once you've read it once, use it as a manual and reference guide so you can constantly use this information for your expansion.

Even if you only use one aspect of this book, and your life improves, then this book will have done its job.

Frequency Astrology

Frequency Astrology is a tool for you to find your personal frequency, so you can play them out loud and see what comes in for you.

If you can't meditate, let the frequency do it for you. Or, let the frequencies enhance the meditations you are already doing.

Play or invoke your frequencies and/or collective frequency, sit with a candle, and gaze into it to see what happens through your senses, both physical and metaphysical.

Clients who have come from all over the world have had excellent experiences that enable them to understand themselves much more, not just during the session but also in their everyday lives and personal sacred places.

Which is why we want to share this tool.

This won't be the only book. There will be further books for astrologers who speak this language and there will be a practitioner book for those who want to help others use these modalities.

But *this* book is to enable you to understand yourself differently which is why this first book is for everybody.

It will bring up questions and aid you in finding the answer you seek.

This is revolutionary, the next step in human evolutionary design.

These are big words and big promises and to experience them, we must open ourselves up and realise that we *can* create our reality. This book will help you understand how to access the fantastic *new normal* that is you.

There are 19 Frequencies.

Just as there are 19 planets, nodes and asteroids, there are 19 frequencies.

All energy centres hold *all* frequencies just like all planets and asteroids within our solar system. As our consciousness expands, we will be aware of more energy centres, planets, nodes, and asteroids.

By looking to your energy centre, you can find your planet, and then, looking at your natal astrology chart, find this planet on the wheel; this tells you the frequency of your energy centre which is the influencer you can tune into to find information to help you. It enables synchronicity to manifest what you've been trying to bring into reality.

At the unique time, place, and date you were born, you brought in these energetic influencers to aid you on your life's journey. This unique energetic influence created your astrological bar code of frequency.

Let me explain that a little more.

The planets within our solar system are like radio stations, sending out information; you are like the radio tuned in to a certain frequency, and depending on what influencers you have chosen depends on the information you tune in to. In other words, there are better radio stations *for you* than others. These radio stations assist you on this journey and during this lifetime.

You brought in these frequencies as you chose the life you are living and the life ahead. The lessons, the work, the loves, the joy, and the exit plan are all coded in this frequency.

Now let's explore your inner solar system.

After learning astrology as a language, it quickly became apparent to me that it was not just planets, asteroids, constellations, stars, and points in the solar system, it began much closer to home, within each of us.

Frequency is in everything. Colour, Sight, Feel, Hearing, Smell, Touch and Taste.

We are entering a time of a new sense, the sight of the third light.

to see BEYOND,
to hear BEYOND,
to smell BEYOND,
to taste BEYOND.

This is the new normal.

FREQUENCY IS A KEY,
CONSCIOUSLY OPEN YOUR FIELD,
THROUGH LOVE AND COMPASSION

The Inner Solar System

The inner solar system is within your energetic centres, littered throughout your body. It is a way of connecting to your consciousness, or your *field*.

Your field is roughly 8 metres all around you and like a mobile phone, it is a magnetic field that attracts frequencies and signals. These signals are what you *need* for *this* journey of your life.

In the case of your field of consciousness, you are connected to the outer planets which send signals to you.

This can be known as your *higher self*.

Our *higher self* is the part of us that could not fit into our physical body but is still very much a part of who we are. We simply could not fit all of who we are, within the physical body, as we would vibrate too much, this is simple physics.

However, we are all still connected through this field. To put it simply, we have a collective field and a personal field.

Let me explain.

Wi-Fi, or radio signals, are an example of the global collective field. Then a mobile phone or a personal radio is an example of the personal field that *connects* to the Wi-Fi. This is why we need time for our personal field to calibrate with the collective field.

As when we are in a collective space with other physical bodies or when we are connected to the same network by mobile phones, we amplify and energize, but when we are not connected, we become fatigued and need a rest, as our field needs to be re-calibrated.

We all do it, some consciously but many unconsciously and simply can be felt by our intuition of knowing that something feels good or off.

Some people *speak* directly to their field; some *feel*, some *hear*, and some *see* but either way, we all have this tool.

So how do we connect?

Simple, through frequency. This is how we tune into our personal mobile phone or radio.

Making sense, yes?

You have numbers within these energy centres that are frequency, sounds, and vibrations within energy centres; once you know these numbers, you play and see what comes in for you; these numbers will guide you in all aspects of your life from health, family, and wealth to work.

Pain is also a signal directed towards you personally trying to get you back on track with your journey and your life.

For instance, pain in your knees can be associated with a fear of moving forward so once you get this message, the frequency will direct you towards what you need such as diet, exercise, medication or whatever will help you to move forward without fear, and without fear, you will release the pain ,as pain is no longer needed ,as a signal. So, it will stop.

To look further into this, I can recommend the excellent book *You Can Heal Your Life* by Louise Hay.

The outer solar system is connected to your energy centres through these numbers which are frequencies (sounds). All we need is the key ,which is the language of astrology which you can learn now. We may not have been ready before, and likely still had life lessons to experience up until this point but now our consciousness is ready for this key.

So, through the exact day, time, and place, you were born, you chose the frequency that you wanted to bring in with you.

Yes, *you* chose; this is where you begin to be empowered.

And this life you are living *isn't* your first ,because death doesn't exist. It's just a change of worlds and dimensions.

I know this is a *big* statement, but we are now moving into a time and a consciousness of KNOWING and the more we see, feel, and hear things that are literally out of this world. All we must do is trust ourselves to *know* what we know now.

There is no going back.

So where do we start on this journey?

Frequency Astrology is one way you can start. As there are many different tools, you need to find just one to get started. This will then attract different tools you need for this life and this journey.

We are moving into a consciousness and field that will use physics and chemistry, rather than a field where we have just been using chemistry.

So, we can now bring the two sciences together. In fact, it's already happening.

This field becomes less outwardly physical and more inwardly elegant.

Frequency Astrology, is a limitless tool to be used to assist you through day-to-day living, meditation and connection which aids your healing.

So, the good news is that you can truly go within for personal answers on your personal journey which helps you find your *line*, or your *path*. When you know how to come back to this line, you can't become lost.

To move forward with this, please have your personal frequency chart made to know all your personal frequencies.Go to dragonseyehub.com for this . Once you start using it, you will see how magnetically your personal field becomes with the collective field. Through synchronicity within the collective field, like a mobile phone with a perfect signal, everything becomes crystal clear, and you start to see people, places and things that may have always been there, but now you can experience them. You will start to draw them all to you by simply having a better signal.

Then, you will start to become aware and wake up to the most amazing and energetic being that you are, and we all are. The earth and her field are so magnificent, and through you, the cosmos, and the universe, you too will start to thrive.

This can happen by taking small steps or significant steps (depending on your field, your soul, your journey, and your life)

This is how you start and awaken to who you are and what you are truly capable of.

At first, it will feel magical but will soon become your new normal.

Chapter 1
The Beginning. The Awakening

So, what is the aim of this book?

This book will reveal to you how you can create your best life. It will help you to understand your personal journey and its challenges. It will equip you with the tools to connect with the inner self through astrology, frequency, and vibration by using the energetic centres within your body and its field. It will teach you how the outer planets are within you and how to use them as the tools you brought in with you on the exact date, time and place you were born.

This book will bring astrology alive in your life. More than just in words, this book will add a different and widening perspective on your personal learning journey and life.

The inner solar system is a system of bringing the energetic bodies and the physical body together. We do this through the energetic highways of the physical body, and the field which is 8 metres all around you. Though this can be called the invisible you, it is still very much a part of you.

Just like WIFI, we are learning to tune into the signals and channels that are most helpful to us to be fully connected and receive an energetic message. In the past, this has gone by many names, such as physics, witchcraft, or simply labeling people with special abilities. However, we are now learning that we all have these special abilities...if we know our frequencies.

Using your frequency (the same frequency you brought in with you from birth) is a tool for creation, understanding and healing so you can ride the wave of life with greater ease.

So, where to begin?

By telling you a little more about who I am and where it all began.

I came from two Piscean parents. My father, a deep-sea diver and my mother, a creative person who was always able to find joy and have it find her. Me? Well, I left school, went to college, and became a hairdresser.

I never dreamt of being a hairdresser, but my mother guided me into this profession to pursue a career (or trade) first and then decide what I wanted to do. While training, they asked me if I would consider moving into art and design as I showed a talent for this. However, I was happy with hairdressing by then as I had found a medium to be creative with and make people happy. Hairdressing was a place I could learn a lot about humankind, and it even aroused my interest in psychology.

This path opened many doors, introduced me to many people and enabled me to travel worldwide. I didn't realise it at the time, but I was being guided by the Universe by following my joy, knowing it would take me where I needed to go.

My first boss was a Buddhist. She was an amazingly creative businesswoman. We did a lot of competition work together, and not only did she teach me about being a businesswoman, but she also taught me a lot about life.

I moved on from this job at 21 and began working for another amazing woman in Leeds, UK. She also taught me a lot about business, and I was happy working there.

However, my father passed, and this encouraged me to leave England. I headed for the United States to stay with family in Texas for a few months to 'sort myself out'. I was offered a job in New York. This excited me but meant that I couldn't leave the USA for two years, so I sadly declined and returned to the UK, where I worked for a big hairdressing company. Within a few months, I moved to London and began teaching other hairdressing students myself. I loved sharing my knowledge and seeing people grow. At 24, I was asked to move to Soho to become a specialist teacher in creative colouring. Before I knew it, I was doing shows and seminars worldwide.

Unfortunately, though, I was having so much fun with my work my mother fell sick, and the illness became terminal. I left London, returned home to the North of England, and opened my own hair salon in Leeds. Taking on all the business advice I learned, I opened another salon. Then, my now husband came on board, and the business expanded even more.

By 2004, we had sold the hairdressing business and relocated to the mountains in France full-time.

The consciousness journey had begun.

2012: The Awakening

Just like any normal day, we were getting ready for visitors. A couple who were house hunting had booked to stay with us at our home in France. They were looking for a home in our area and had chosen to stay with us because it was central to their search. They were due to arrive in the afternoon. Me and Martyn (my husband) were having a cuppa (as we say in England), to recuperate from getting the guest room ready and giving the garden a much-needed spring makeover.

There was a knock at the door, and I rushed to greet our guests. Standing there were Emma & Christian and without knowing why, I felt the energy expand at such a rate that it took my breath away. It was as if a loud thunderclap had knocked the wind out of me. Before I had a chance to show them to the guest room, I had learned that Emma was a psychic medium.

Emma looked at me and smiled. She knew that I had just felt something incredibly special. My face must have given it away.

'We need to have a conversation', she said.

I was confused.

As Martyn offered our guests a drink, we sat at the table in our main sitting room. Martyn kept the pleasant conversation going with Christian; however, I couldn't do the same.

'What just happened?', I blurted out.

Emma calmly explained that she was a psychic medium who had been guided to relocate to France and find a new home.

This sounded familiar. It was just what I had done, without consciously knowing it.

We talked for six hours. Though I had never met her before, it was easy to engage in deep conversations about the cosmos, the soul, life, death, the Universe, and everything in between.

This was the start of my consciousness awakening. This was the beginning of the journey that I was about to take.

For the next six weeks my expansion continued. I often found myself saying 'that is so weird' as a response to the mind-blowing nature of our conversations and experiences. Emma guided me to no longer be so surprised about what I was experiencing, and I quickly replaced the word 'weird' with 'amazing', which gave birth to my nickname for my new friend 'Amazing Emma'.

Still, to this day she is saved in my phone as 'Amazing Emma'.

One day, when I was energetically ready, she gave me the greatest gift of all that was her unique meditation that was shown to her by her guide.

From that day forward, I never looked back.

This particular meditation enables your mind to create a place where you can thrive. Regardless of whatever your journey is, this meditation allows you to let go.

It starts with opening your chakras (also known as your energy centres, which we will talk about later in the book). To do this imagine a flower opening petal by petal ,or a box with a door opening ,revealing a color which activates your field within.

* * *

Here are the seven chakras.

1. **Red, root chakra, between your legs in the crotch area**
2. **Orange, sacral chakra, lower belly**
3. **Yellow, solar plexus, top belly**
4. **Pink or green, heart**
5. **Mediterranean blue, throat**
6. **Indigo blue, third eye, in between your eyes, your forehead**
7. **Violet, crown, on top of your head.**

* * *

Once you open your chakras, starting from your root (red), moving up the body, visioning each colour emanating from the flower as the petals open, until you reach the crown (violet) chakra.

It's best to keep your eyes closed.

Let the magic begin

The Meditation

You can listen to this meditation on dragonseyehub.com

Get comfortable, however, that looks for you.

Close your eyes.

Start by opening your chakras.

Then, ask the highest of the high and the gatekeeper, to walk with you and protect you through this meditation.

Now, imagine a gate in front of you. Put your hand out and feel the gate.

How does it feel?

Cold? Warm? Rugged? Smooth?

Pay attention to what you feel with your senses as this practice deepens.

This allows you to get into the theta state, which is the state your brain goes into when driving a car on a familiar route. Though you do not become unconscious, you don't have to actively engage your senses as the body goes into autopilot.

Now, open the gate.

How does it sound?

This is your gate. Remember it.

Now, look to the floor.

There is a path ahead of you which leads you to a bridge.

Step onto this path.

This is your path. Remember it.

Take a moment to observe what your feet look like.

As you start to walk along the path, as yourself, what colour is the path? How do your feet sound when walking on it?

Are you barefoot?

How does it feel?

As you look to the right, you will see a river.

To your left, you will see an embankment of flowers and grass.

Continue to walk and look at the river.

What colour is it?

Is it flowing fast or slow?

Look up to the sky.

What colour is it?

Are there clouds?

Anything else flying up there?

Is the sun out?

As you reach the bridge, take a moment to observe what the bridge looks like.

As you step onto the bridge, feel the side of it.

This is your bridge. Remember it.

Feel the bridge with your hands as you walk to the middle of it.

How does the bridge feel?

As you get to the middle, look over the side into the river.

What can you see?

Can you see a reflection of yourself?

If so, what does that look like?

Now walk to the end of the bridge.

In front of you there is a large field.

In the distance, you can see a big tree, to the right of it, you can see caves, to the left, you can see cliffs, a beach, and the infinite sea.

What does the field look like?

Is it green grass, or wheat, or stone?

Now, take a step into this field and walk towards the tree.

As you get closer, take a moment to observe what the tree looks like.

There will be a seating arrangement by the tree, but for now we will focus on the tree. Walk towards it, can you wrap your arms around it?

How does the bark feel?

How does the tree trunk feel when you run your hands up and down it?

Look up into the tree's canopy now. What do you see?

With the tree behind you, turn around and you'll see a bench or a blanket where you can sit.

Take a seat in the seating area, feel it, inspect it in detail.

On your left, you can see the caves, to the right, you can see the cliff, the beach and the infinite sea beyond. To the right the caves to the left cliffs, beach and the infinite sea beyond.

Take a moment to look at this place.

This is your place, remember it.

Breathe deeply three times, through the nose, then hold for three counts, then exhale three times, doing this three times.

Is there anyone or anything around you?

From where you are sitting, is there a breeze, is it warm, what does this place look like in detail.

The seat is yours; the place is yours, you are safe, and you can enter and leave at any time.

We will sit here until you are ready.

As you stand, walk toward the cliff, on your right, you will see a walkway down to the beach. What does it look like?

Step on the path down to the beach and feel the rock of the cliff on your right-hand side as you walk step by step.

When you reach the bottom of the steps, look at the rock of the cliff, what color is it?

Observe the beach, see what colour the sand is, take a step, does it feel fine or coarse, warm, or cold, wet, or dry, how does the beach feel to you?

Now we are going toward the sea, does it look calm or rough, does it have clear water, is there anything in it, like fish?

Let's take a seat on the beach, how does it feel to sit there?

Looking out at the beach, remember this is your beach, you are always safe here.

When you have taken three deep breaths through your nose, out through your mouth, count to three inwards, hold, then count to three, then exhale. Once you are ready, stand up and walk back up the cliff.

At the top, you can see caves ahead, which you can explore when you're ready.

This is your place; you can come here anytime. To the left are the trees and the bench, to the right the bridge, remember this is your place, you are welcome to come here at any time.

Let's walk towards the bridge, as you take each step, does anything change, or does it remain the same? Look up at the sky, again has it changed or is it the same?

Ask yourself the same questions as you approach the bridge.

Go to the middle of the bridge, look over, and ask the same questions.

Remember this place is your safe place as you walk to the end of the bridge, to the footpath.

Step onto the path, has it changed? Up ahead, you'll see your gate as you turn left.

When you step onto the path, does it look different or the same as before?

Have a look at the river on your left. How does it look?

Ask the same questions as you approach the gate.

Upon opening the gate, look over your left shoulder, remember the path, this is your path, see the river, this is your river, and observe the bridge, this is your bridge.

Once you have opened the gate, close it behind you.

This is the time to close your chakras, your energy centres used for meditation.

You can now reverse this action, and close them, just like we opened them. Imagine the top of your head to be a flower or box.

Color by colour, starting at the top of your head and working your way down.

The colors are violet, indigo, blue, green, pink, yellow, orange, then red.

You can now thank the highest of the high and the gatekeeper, they can leave now.

After you have done this meditation, perhaps you can write down what you saw, smelled, felt, and any changes you noticed.

Keep crystals in your hand or place them by your side.

This meditation can be done anywhere, anytime.

In writing this meditation, I give thanks to Emma, all the guides I've worked with, and myself.

* * *

As I started the meditation, I opened the gate, and walked on to the path.

Walking next to me was a foot belonging to my first-ever spirit guide (in this life), Sam, who gently guided me through the basics while emanating love, crystals, light, light people and how we are all one.

Then he asked me to write all the meditations in a book.

'The book will come to me', he said.

It was right there on my bedside when I emerged from meditation. How amazing.

So, I wrote down every meditation just as I was coming out of it, as you remember everything when you have just come out.

This was the beginning of my remembering. It was a love affair, he is amazing, I still have the little book of meditations, which I will one day publish.

A Channeled Message

Egypt, a time when all galactic powers
came to Gaia, to many portals over
Gaia, to regenerate and connect their
Universes to her frequencies.

Pyramids were energy (frequency)
transformers from the earth to her
crystal dimension within her, to the
great central sun, via our planets.

All who lived around them thrived and
there was no dis-ease.

All were joyful.

In Egypt, it was so green, going as far as the
Sahara Desert and beyond. Green so
green and it all thrived as the
frequencies were enabling this.

Pyramids all over the earth were allowing
for this.

All were happy, thriving, and joyful on this
emotional belt.

*Many schools were there, they showed me
the school of the sphinx, so green
underneath and all around, with long
steps encircling her when you reached
the top of the step. There is a huge base,
with steps going underneath to many
rooms, where gatherings took place
where knowledge was shared.*

*On my astrological natal chart, they
showed me where we learned about our
frequency on earth, where they showed
you how to make your own frequency
grid so you can thrive.*

*By playing your frequencies to different
energy centres, you can rebalance.*

*Through power, the emotional belt got
stuck, held on a loop.*

*Through Egypt, the galactic gradually left,
the energy frequencies were too dense,
so the galactic who were resting left.*

*The reincarnation of many has helped this
rectification, through love and*

remembrance of these times, to aid and
restore.

An important date: 21st December 2020.

This winter solstice marks the darkest
night of the year. Jupiter and Saturn
will be conjunct in the western sky,
creating a portal for many energies to
flood the planet and all living
things...the clock is ticking, can it stop?

Green bliss, White light.

Which will be here throughout 2021-2023.

Planets in your cosmos allow frequency to
enter, flow, and then leave, which
allows all of us to grow and learn.

Chapter 2
How Do We Connect?

We now know that we connect through meditation, but there are many other tools we can connect with. As we expand and evolve so does our 'tool kit'.

Inner solar systems are like outer solar systems, but inside our field, we are a galaxy. The inner solar system consists of energy centres, planets, and frequencies. It then receives messages from our cosmos AKA the outer solar system.

Sounds too easy, right?

Well, that's because it is, but only once you get used to working with it.

All you need is your astrological chart, and we'll show you how to connect it to your inner solar system.

It all becomes very easy to use once you have all your personal frequencies, for your own energy centres, on your Personal Astrological Frequency Chart.

Just play and see what comes in, just like a radio.

You can have a chart made up with all your personal frequencies at dragonseyehub.com

As planets, asteroids, and points move around our cosmos constantly sending us messages, we can connect with them.

How do you use it?

By playing the frequency of, let's say, the moon.

You look at your personal moon frequency, play it, sit quietly for 10 minutes, 20 minutes or more, whatever you feel is right for you and see what happens for you. It will help you relax; it will help you meditate if you meditate, it will help you calm down, it will help you cope with anxiety, and it will help you heal physically and mentally,through emotional wisdom. Play for as long as you feel it is right for you, let the synchronicity play out, you will become more aware of the world around you, and you may have epiphanies as you go about your day.

The moon is in your solar plexus energy centre (your top belly), on the left-hand side.

The more you understand where this energy comes from within the physical body, the more you will understand why you feel a certain way.

Playing the frequency shifts things in your personal world, allowing your perspective to shift.

You begin to understand, the real reasons for things happening in your life, and in your world.

In addition, this realizes physical healing within the body, as healing isn't just physical, but has many layers. This allows insight into being, you realize it into being. You don't have to believe in anything, it just attracts what you need.

This is why this book has come into realization.

I play mine at least once a day since this is just the beginning. It will be expanded upon over time, over the next millennium, by many.

We're just getting started...

The galactic symbol of unity came to me in a vision one day when I was getting out of the shower whilst visiting Romania. It was right in front of me, made purely of white light and I had no idea what it was. I opened the door to see if it was a reflection but there was nothing. I looked above, I looked below, and I looked all over the room to see where it might be coming from, but there was nothing.

I had to trust that this was the moment when the energy manifested into the physical.

When I returned home, it all became clear, and I was intuitive about how to use it. Then I realized that I was channeling conscious energy, as my energy field had changed.

All the information that I had been working with since 2012 came together which created **Frequency Astrology, A Tool for All.**

But, where to start?

What is Gaia and the Inner Solar System?

There is planet Earth, a solid mass of all things, and all things have consciousness, a magnetic field. The consciousness, the magnetic field, of our earth is called GAIA.

In this physical world, your inner solar system can be viewed through the chakras that run throughout your physical body. It is a way to connect to your consciousness, in a more physical way.

All your energy centres contain numbers that are frequencies, sounds, vibrations,light codes . When you know these numbers, you simply play or invoke and see what comes in. These numbers will guide you in all aspects of your life from health to family to wealth.

In this moment, the outer solar system is connected to your energy-field, your consciousness, that is roughly 8 metres all around you. This is magnetic energy, just as the field of our planet, earth, is Gaia, her consciousness.

Water conducts all this energy around the body because our bodies are electric, just like the earth.

The outer solar system connects to your field, through which, then connects to your physical body, then to your energy centres, of which you have many.

There are numbers associated with each energy centre, which are frequencies. We didn't have all the information at the beginning, as consciousness (our field) wasn't ready. We were still tasting different scenarios for our soul's learning but now our consciousness is ready for this key.

Magnetic & Tachyon Energy

This book has a polarizing ability, which is mostly invisible to the human eye, which attracts and deflects what is needed for your journey. Using 'un-frequenced' energy from the Universe, we create within our energetic field a code that we brought with us on the day, time, and place of our birth.

A Channeled Message: The slip ©

*The wolf, Harry, came to me this morning
at 4.30 am. He is very big, his hair is
rough, and he is very gentle.*
*I was shown The Slip again. On this slip,
everything is composed of numbers.
Like computer code.*

*Next, we went to the colour ray of violet.
This color is of a vibration of the 3 and
is why healers use this colour. This is
where the physical body lives. This is
where you can change the composition
of the numbers found in The Slip. And
when they change, there is a physical
change within you. This is where we
really learn to co-create, not heal
necessarily, but to change the coding
within and without the body.*

*When a certain frequency is used, the
numbers within that frequency
resonate with the physical to recompose
the numbers to then change it.*

We are reprogramming our body the same

way a technician would reprogram a computer.

If you look at violet beyond light, you see nothing physical, so you become molecules and can flow like a stream of numbers. In effect, you become a sound wave, which appears to consist of trillions of numbers when you look closely. I can travel anywhere as a sound wave and become anything as a result.

During my time on Bear Island, Harry taught me how to meditate and enter the 'limitless' through utilizing Dolphin Energy. I did this by imagining a dolphin holding their fin and traveling through the water. I did this until the limitless appeared. You can also enter the limitless by using this dolphin energy meditation.

I stepped off the dolphin and sat down on Bear Island. There was nothing but blue sky, clear beaches, and water. I put my hands to my third eye, palm side up, and let go. We meditated

within meditation, then again within
meditation. This is the number 3.

We made The Slip here; the flow of
numbers came out of the palms of the
hands like heat coming from a hot pie,
waves, and waves of numbers. The Slip
appeared, like a tear in the fabric of
what I saw in front of me, and you just
slipped into it. That's how we created
it, the slip in time, the portal, the
gateway.

Everything was in reverse. I traveled
through light into the dark, as if I was
falling backwards. I could see
everything in reverse, all the colours,
within the white, then I simply became
molecules and decomposed into
everything (in a matter of seconds).

So, if you go there with a client and use
frequency for composition, the same
way you compose music, then you
come forward through the colours, then
through The Slip, then you've created.

Intention is vital because by the frequency

*of your words, you are composing...you
are co-creating.*

*The physical on this plane is created by
trillions of molecules flowing as you go
through your daily life. Every word has
a frequency, a number composition.*

*Now we can play with the numbers and
the frequency on a conscious level.*

*The frequency that we call fate, is the
frequency you are programmed to use
,to create the numbers within the
frequency, to create life, to create
learning.*

*But what it is, just experiences because it is
trillions of numbers recomposing in a
millisecond.*

*So, let's break it down through the heart
space through the third eye.*

*Imagine everything as number code and
learn to compose how those number
codes form through the frequency of
words. This is why mantras and*

*affirmation are so important. This is
also why colour is important because it
is a frequency. A great metaphor here is
'painting by numbers' as with painting
one of these designs, soon the number
disappears and the perfect image is
formed as if, underneath, there is no
number code at all. The patterns and
images these number codes can form is
limitless.*

*This is the flow which when it moves, we
call time. We can slow it down, stop it,
then it goes backwards, and move it in
any direction. Amazing right?*

*If you go in any direction from a number (a
point), you are going beyond time and
into the colour code. This is how you
can create anything.*

*When you close your eyes, imagine in
numbers, then go within the numbers,
or colors, then go within the colours, or
waves, then go within the waves. This
is what we mean by going within; to go
within the code.*

It is only when you go within that you can create anything. Then you can un-create, or transition from one thing to another. This is why death does not exist in human terms.

0 and 1 is matter.
2 is frequency.
3 is light.
4 is movement.

Chapter 3
Energy Centres, Planets and Frequency

The inner solar system is made up of three components, which are; Energy centres, Planets and Frequencys.

Your energy centres are wheels of energy that spiral around certain points of the body, directing energy. The ancients used the word chakra to refer to these centres, a term you are probably familiar with. I will use these terms interchangeably throughout the book.

Through meditation, I was shown that each Chakra had a planet, a major planet that drives its energy, like a mini solar system.

All frequencies exist within each energy centre. Also, each energy centre has a dedicated frequency and a major frequency, which drives its energy.

As shown on the next page, all living things have energy centres. A complete list of their locations on the body is included.

In 2016, I began researching the oracle of frequency, not knowing what it would lead to, but finding it fascinating, which is when I discovered the correlation between energy centres and frequency.

You may know that there are seven chakras, but for this tool, we have developed the model to contain twelve energy centres. They start at about 10 cm below your feet and work upwards.

ENERGY CENTERS OF THE INNER SOLAR SYSTEM

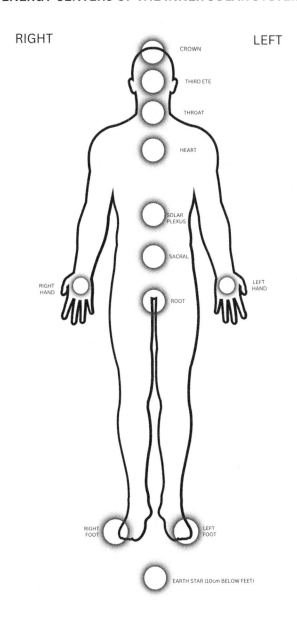

A list of the human body's energy centres.

- Earth star, (located below your feet ,1 o cm approx.)
- Left foot energy centre.
- Right foot energy centre
- Root energy centre (located in your crotch area)
- Sacral energy centre (located in the lower belly)
- Solar plexus energy centre (located in the top belly area)
- Heart energy centre (located in the heart area, middle of the chest, and spanning out)
- Left-hand energy centre.
- Right-hand energy centre.
- Throat energy centre (located on the throat)
- Third eye energy centre (located middle of your forehead, between the eyes)
- Crown energy centre (located at the top of the head)

Planets

Each energy centre has a dedicated planet within it.

I took an astrology course in 2o1 9, after the exams, I was instructed by my guides to forget everything I thought I knew of astrology (which I did), and then I was introduced to electromagnetic energy centres, frequency and planets.

It was a game changer.

This field was not linear or black and white, but instead was quantum and multidimensional, nevertheless also being elegant and beautifully designed.

It taught me that for the particular journey of life we are on, there are dominant frequencies that are required which are based on the planet or solar system we are on.

Here are the dominant planets needed for the Gaia experience, just like we need different ingredients to make a cake, some more dominant than others.

A list of planets that correspond to energy centres.

- Earth star .... ceres
- Left foot ...Venus.
- Right foot ...Mars
- Root ...Jupiter
- Sacral .... Sun
- Solar Plexus ...Moon, Mercury
- Heart .... Neptune, Chiron
- Left hand ...Venus.
- Right hand ...Mars
- Throat.... Pluto
- Third Eye .... Saturn, Uranus
- Crown .... Poseidon

So how do the planets work within and outside our bodies, fields, and cosmos?

In another meditation, I was guided to connect with Venus. This surprised me since I consider myself more of a Jupiter girl than a Venus girl.

With astrology and inner searching, the moon seems to be guiding us, so I swayed towards it to, as do many.

Afterwards, a team of guides (I refer to them as The Council of the Three) revealed that we are moving into a time when we will be more connected to our higher self, which is a part of our whole soul that could not fit into a three-dimensional body.

Connecting to all our bodies and not just the physical, creates a harmonizing rhythm which produces a more sovereign perspective. Here, the decisions we make are our own, balanced with the collective of our outside world. Not the other way around.

'What does that mean?', I asked, they explained,

Over thousands of years, we have ceded all our sovereignty to others. For instance, if something goes wrong in these times, we tend to blame an outside source rather than look within, seeing what is troubling us, whether it is a situation, an illness, etc. This was a very valuable lesson.

As we move into these times we must go within and ask ourselves the question 'what is needed' and 'what am I learning through this?' Then we can ask, 'what can I do to enable myself to open up to synchronicity?'. By doing this, you will begin to see what comes knocking at your door and will have the insight to choose what is best for you in that particular moment at that particular time.

True Sovereignty: Frequency (Vibration/ Code)

A picture of the collective frequency used within the 12 energy centres can be seen below, as we discussed within each energy centre there is a dedicated planet and frequency.

All of which are brought together within.

The 12 Oracles

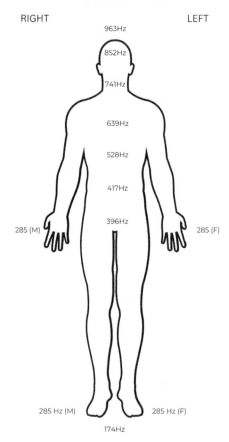

UNCONSCIOUS COLLECTIVE FREQUENCIES
OF THE INNER SOLAR SYSTEM

RIGHT   LEFT

963Hz
852Hz
741Hz
639Hz
528Hz
417Hz
396Hz

285 (M)   285 (F)

285 Hz (M)   285 Hz (F)
174Hz

- **Earth star, 174 Hz:** This is used for release ,
  physical pain, for connecting with mother earth,
  and to heal you. This can also be used for
  collective grounding, for example in a group

session. For these evolving times, finding your personal earth star is like finding your personal painkiller.

- **Left foot, 285 Hz:** This frequency is the collective connection, the frequency of receiving energy, from the earth and to each other. The frequency of the collective balance is also the frequency of the collective feminine divine energy. If you play this frequency and have problems with the left foot or left side of your body, it will help you as well. You can gain an easy translation for your journey when you find your personal Venus. A place of balance.

- **Right foot, 285 Hz:** Besides being the frequency of connecting to collective release, this is also the frequency of collective balance. When you find your personal mars,this is a place of balance, this will enable your energy, give you the fuse to ignite your personal fire. It is the collective male divine energy.

- **Root, 396 Hz:** A frequency of collective expansion connects to the feet and the earth star. It is known as the earth diamond frequency. Playing these 4 frequencies will activate the collective earth diamond, where expansion, balance, connection, and release can be found. Discovering your personal roots will allow you to expand on what you already know, and move forward to soul growth, the purpose of your life.

- **Sacral, 417 Hz:** There is a collective creative frequency energy there, which enables collective flow, and it enables the access to the collective creative consciousness and the creator consciousness. You will be able to express yourself creatively when you find your personal sun. You will be able to create through whatever medium you choose when you find your personal sun.

- **Solar plexus, 528 Hz:** With this frequency, you can access the collective consciousness mind, empathy, emotional intellegence, and the feel sensation of the collective. You will be able to work with your conscious mind, bringing in what you need with your reflective emotions, to feel your way through, with true self-empathy and compassion, with what is within your conscious mind.

- **Heart, 639 Hz:** The collective heart is the healing frequency of the collective, you can play this in your house, around all living things, in clinics, doctors' surgeries, hospitals, etc. Within our field and out of our field, you can connect to the consciousness of our solar system in a limitless manner, as well as release collective energy that is no longer needed. The release of karma, working with the ancestral collective energy, can be used to connect the collective heart-mind coherence, through your own. By saying the affirmation and playing this frequency, you can put intention into the collective soup, through your field, enter the collective heart space, and place intention there. This is conscious work, as we do unconsciously every day when we talk or think. When you find your personal Chiron and Neptune, this is the bridge frequency to release what no longer needs to be kept, and to bring in, to get you ready, to connect through the throat of change, to the realm of the third eye, the true manifestation of your soul growth, your new road, your self-evolution.

- **Left hand, 285 Hz / Right hand, 285 Hz:** As your earth diamond connects to your left hand and right hand, you can manually work with this frequency, by laying on the hands, with the left hand for receiving and the right hand for releasing. When we place on our body or on others, when we hug, shake hands, stroke pets, if we know which hand we are using, then we can consciously enable this frequency.

- **Throat, 741 Hz:** Through speech, we can enable the collective to speak their truths and be heard, which is great for schools and auditoriums. This frequency will help you if you are making a speech, this also detoxifies and transforms, this frequency will help when collective change for the highest good is required. By knowing your own Pluto, you can speak your truth with love and be heard. You can play or activate this when you are in a situation where you need to be heard, within any environment, this is where you can truly connect to the heart-brain coherence, where what no longer serves you is liberated, a transformation can begin.

- **Third Eye, 852 Hz:** If you want to activate your collective third-eye energy, this frequency is good for think tanks, group settings, or brainstorming. A collective psychic energy, limitless vision, and limitless manifestation, you must see it before you build it. When you know your third personal eye, you can connect to your subconscious, where forgiveness of self and others can be made, using compassion of the heart, where you will find the true reason for the great lessons that lie there, you can move your energy, on to the revolutionary, liberating, evolutionary, conscious new road that you are embarking on, not only for you, but for the whole of Gaia's consciousness. Whenever you forgive yourself and others, within your own knowledge, you enable others to feed into this, and it becomes the new norm.

- **Crown, 963 Hz:** Play this frequency and connect to the collective consciousness. This is the collective frequency of connection. By connecting to the collective higher self, you will be able to connect outside and within your field. This frequency is very good for meditation, as it helps you reach the collective theta state. Once you know your personal crown, you will know what you are connecting to, once you know your personal frequency of this energy centre and the energy centres beyond this lifetime.

The collective frequencies v personal frequencies

To connect with the collective frequencies (fields) of consciousness, we have provided you with a list. You can use these frequencies to ask questions or to receive an answer.

Your personal frequencies are the ones you brought with you when you were born based on the exact time, date, and place of your birth (if you do not have the exact time, we use 12 midday for the average).

You can have your personal frequency chart made and sent to you at dragonseyehub.com, where you can get a full explanation of what it means for you.

As soon as you have your personal frequency chart, you will be able to connect with your own conscious frequencies, your field, and then you will be able to go within, ask personal questions, and retrieve your own personal answers, for your own conscious journey, so you can learn more about yourself.

We talked about you being your mobile phone or similar device, so using this same analogy, your personal frequencies are your phone number and your email address that directly connect to you/ your device. This is so you can receive personal messages, rather than the collective frequency. Imagine how unpleasant it would be if your mobile phone was picking up all the text messages and phone calls in your area. You would get too much information that wasn't personal to you. Personal frequencies, as the name implies, are totally personal to you and no one else.

If a full moon or new moon occurs in our galaxy or a conjunction happens between planets, or even if a planet, asteroid, or point in a specific place aspect your personal planets, you can tune in using your frequency, and find out what that certain frequency personally means for you on your journey.

Affirmations, which are like instructions, will light up the frequency.

During mediation in 2018, I was shown to train in BQH regression hypnotherapy I followed the instructions which led me to knowing. Since 2012, my world has been turned upside down (in a good way) by the teaching of Dolores Canon. I was guided to read the work of this teacher by my soul friend Emma, and I am deeply grateful I did.

My own regression was amazing. When I started the course, I took part in a session which revealed lives in other Universes working with frequency. This was not something I was aware of at the time.

After I began practising regression hypnotherapy, I discovered that all I had read and channeled over the previous years was coming truer and truer for me as I experienced at least twenty-five personal encounters with other souls on the frequency level.

Now I want to know more.

When I asked the cosmos, 'Where do we start? And 'How do we connect? they answered, 'frequency is an extremely good tool'.

And so, the journey began.

Astrology and the planets are our language, so we can communicate and connect clearer with frequency. We do this through affirmation and meditation.

For meditation, you can do everything from a classic meditation to bathing, walking, running or candle gazing. Whatever you need to do to let go of your daily thoughts and clear your mind, so you are open to receive messages from your higher self.

What is a Higher Self?, you may ask.

It is the parts of your soul that couldn't fit into this three-dimensional human vehicle called your body.

For example, suppose you had a wardrobe full of body suits, from all over the Universe, and for this lifetime you chose this particular body from your wardrobe for this particular journey and set of lessons. However, all of you cannot fit into the body suit so you leave the bigger part of you, the Higher Self in non-psychical form. However, this part of you never stops being part of you. It just isn't in the suit. You see, all of your past lives and all the dimensions and planets from all over the Universes are stored in the higher self. The higher self has all the information from all the billions of years you have been a soul.

But how do we connect with your higher self?

By listening to our inner voice. That 'gut' feeling you can connect with at any time (if you wish). As I was shown the inner solar system, they explained that all the outer planets are connected to your body via energy centres and frequencies.

Once again, imagine a mobile phone. This device is you. You are your hard drive set at certain frequencies for this life you lead right now. You are your energy centres, these mini solar systems constantly picking up messages around you. A message is picked up through your wireless network. We all have a mobile phone, or we've seen one, and we know it works, but most of us have no idea how it works.

This is how your field works, just like WIFI.

Just like wifi, your field is connecting to masts with large dishes from various companies, which channel signals to and from the satellites to the servers. The server being Source (your higher self) where we live as souls.The satellites being the planets . It is a difficult one to understand this with our logic and linear brain, so we hope this book helps you to understand things in a different way.

With the outer planets, you can understand, through the language of astrology and frequency, how we can learn and grow through constant change for our soul growth. With the outer planets of our solar system, we can see into the future possibilities through cyclical events and subsequently prepare so when something happens, we can simply sit back and watch it unfold as opposed to being in chaos or crisis. With astrology and frequency, we can see what it means for you individually (or collectively) based on the frequency played, by using astrology and frequency. Accordingly, you can then enable frequency with affirmations and intentions.

By tuning into the frequencies associated with certain planets and constellations, you can connect and receive messages from your field. More importantly, you can experience the synchronicity that your higher self is trying to show you.

We all regret, at some point in our lives, not listening to ourselves when we had a, for lack of a better word, 'feeling' about it. This can be called our inner knowing. When we decide to listen to an outside source instead of listening to ourselves, we can often be swayed, even with the best logic, out of our highest good or unfolding. Knowing this doesn't mean that you should then sway others' decisions by giving them knowledge of their inner knowing but to understand for yourself that you must first know yourself and then go out into the world, share, talk, debate, and grow.

Other people may also be helpful in listening to your inner knowing because when you don't have the answer someone else might trigger something within you with their insight, opinion, or information. This is synchronicity, and you can use it to move forward.

The key to all of this is to make decisions from your inner knowing, then gather outside information.

Using your inner compass and solar system you can become more discerning with a lot of confusion in today's world. You see, the purpose of so many of us being here on planet earth, right now, is to assist in this consciousness shift which will allow the dynamics of our own fields to shift. We are literally here to aid the movement of the entire world forward. In fact, we are all part of this magnificent shift, however, some of us know it consciously. We and all make this planet so wonderful and offer lessons for each of us to learn and grow in so many ways. Therefore, we learn from every perspective. There is no good or bad which means we need not judge others so harshly as their actions are allowing us to learn and grow even more. There is a field shift occurring on the planet, including everything on it, above it, and within it. At the moment, we are working in an 8-metre field, we will evolve to a 12-metre field, then eventually to a 16-metre field, which will take approximately 440 years to complete as time moves forward. There is a constant shift, a quickening in timelines, so this may change.

We are at the beginning, sowing the seeds, then coming back (incarnating)or staying the same(within the same body), it depends on you and your soul path.

Along the way, why not have some soul-stirring experiences?

There's no doubt that uncomfortable situations teach us more than lying on a beach.

I asked, "How does the solar system work?" As this is for everyone, I kept it simple. They started the conversation from there. Our discussion started with what each planet gives energetically, so we talked about astrology.

A Channeling: 4,8,12,16 The evolutionary numerological code for unity.

There are 16 circles spiralling out from the world, all of which correspond to Universal lines in all the universes. All things in your world are connected by a crystalline line, these are the evolutionary lines.

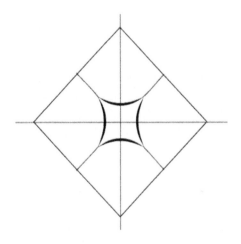

In it, 16 circles spiral out and 4 lines cross, which are the lines of the world in which you reside, Gaia, The Pearl.

There are four more lines crossing, these are the universal lines that connect Gaia to all the other Universes.

These are the Crystalline lines that connect

all things in your world, these are the evolutionary lines.

This is the Pentagon, the human design, which is the line of creation and manifestation.

Human manifestation is contained within this.

This is your inner solar system.

This consists of energy centres, frequencies, and planets.

As you use this map, you will come to realise what you are supremely capable of.

When the planets in your outer world cross these lines, you can connect to the crystalline grid and all things within it. You can connect to all Universes; you can connect to your world.

If you know your inner frequencies, you can use them as a tool.

*It is important to connect with your world,
your crystalline grid, and the Universe
to resonate with them.*

*The home of frequency astrology is
channeled for the new awakening field
of consciousness.*

*In Frequency Astrology, you are connected
to the Pearl, the Earth, the solar system,
and all the Universes.*

Chapter 4
Astrology, A Simple Guide

So here we go.

Below is the astrology chart.

You chose a specific time, date, and place to be born to best aid you on this journey that we call life.

In the below circle, there are 12 even quadrants, as many as months there are in a year. The circle contains 360 degrees, approximately the same as there are days in a year, and 30 degrees in each quadrant, approximately as there are roughly days in a month. Despite not exactly following the calendar year, this is an accurate way to code energy cycles for personal use.

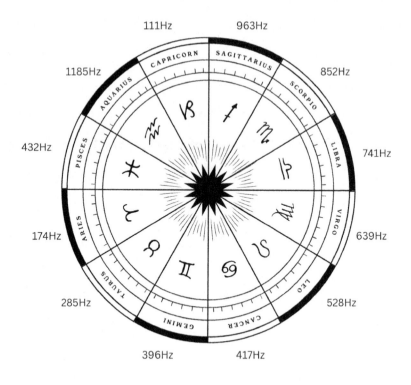

As soon as you are born, the planets that surround the earth are logged at certain points, as if they were a photo taken at that very moment. All degrees and minutes of each planet are logged in this circle, forming the basis of your natal chart - a unique document, a blueprint, that is only for you. It will be slightly different to those who were born on the same day as you at different times and in different locations.

For example, your personal chart (also known as a natal chart) shows items in degrees and minutes. The laws of

84

astrology say that when a degree passes 30 minutes, it becomes the next degree. So, for example, if your chart shows Pluto at 18 degrees and 31 minutes ,you can round it up to 19 degrees .

There are 12 sections, each of which contains 30 degrees. Various astrologers divide and use the degrees differently. To keep things simple, we use 00.00 degrees to 29 degrees in each section, followed by 30.00 degrees to 59.00 degrees in the next section. As there is a border between each section, we continue to work around until we reach 360 degrees.

With the help of specific planets, within this galaxy, you will be able to receive specific frequencies, which will allow you to align yourself with specific people, places, environment, tastes, smells, and choices. These specific things enable you to learn and grow on your personal journey and assist the entire planet in its collective journey. A journey from the unknown to the known occurs at this point. Where is your Jupiter located, for instance?

Your root energy centre contains Jupiter for you as a human. Currently, the planet Jupiter is tuned in. Jupiter is the planet of expansion, your root energy centre,(we know when a plant grows, it needs the root to expand) that yearns to expand, since the point of being born is to learn and grow. Jupiter is all about expansion.

On your chart, find Jupiter, find the constellation, which will tell us the frequency, then find the degree, which will tell us how many beats the constellation frequency has.

As soon as we know Jupiter's frequency, we know our root energy centre frequency, so we can use this frequency to earth our energy, to use magnetic energy fused with electrical energy for healing, to meditate on, to enable us to expand, whatever we wish to do, within our root energy centre. This is the root that will grow in this lifetime, and it will vibrate out to all other energy centres, which creates a domino effect.

Whenever Jupiter is conjunct or in a particular place, it will affect your root energy centre, your growth, and your expansion in this lifetime.

As Jupiter moves through the cosmos, it will send messages every nanosecond to your root energy centre! You can play your personal root energy frequency as Jupiter moves, sit back, and see what comes in for you and your journey.

This is where astrology becomes very personal, intimate, and empowering.

The Planets

For our three-dimension minds to grasp the concept and purpose of our planets, I have crafted a quick and easy guide for reference. Even though I have given each planet he/she pronoun, all planets are both masculine and feminine in nature.

- **The Sun**: The Sun, also known as the great illuminator within us receives messages from the great central Sun far past the Milky Way. Some call this the 'God Voice', which is why we are all gods, as some people say. The Sun is what is known as **The Divine** and **The I Am**. It is our Creative Source. Our sun receives the messages, then sends them out in our solar system.
- **Mercury**: Mercury receives messages as he is our Conscious Mind which makes us aware of the message . As we are all on different journeys, these messages will mean different things to different energy types (human, animal, sea, etc.)
- **Venus:** Venus is the translator of energy. She deciphers the messages into energy that we can see, feel, hear, and touch. She can translate it for you to understand. All you have to do is connect with her.
- **Earth:** It is on Earth that the translations of Venus are transformed into a three-dimensional world (field), where they manifest into a structured matter. In this space, the energy takes

on a different vibration and a different form of energy as it has been given structure.

- **Mars:** There is no question that Mars is the Divine force as it gives everything energy. It is the starter energy, the life force energy; that boost, that kick, that jump-start, the heat, the fire, and the passion running along our lives.

- **Jupiter:** The expansive energy is the energy that wants you to grow and widen your perspective. The same way air is given to a deflated balloon, He will give it air to you so that you can grow bigger than you were before.

- **Saturn, Your Dragon:** The teacher energy of Saturn is the creator of worlds, fields, numbers, code, and sacred geometry. He is the catalyst for co-creation and manifestation.

- **Uranus :** Uranus represents universal change, the new road so to speak. It is the lightning bolt moment that creates a 90 ° turn down a new path. In this energy, you can anticipate his presence, but how it manifests is something you don't see coming. That is different. You might say, *'wow, I didn't see that coming'*. This is what some might call fate, kismet, predestination, or preordained. Pushing against this energy will not be an easy road.

- **Neptune:** Neptune represents the limitless. He is limitless love. He is limitless consciousness. He is the field, without boundaries. He says 'why walk when you can fly, why fly when you can soar. He wants you to explore, explore, explore, and just let go.

- **Pluto:** As Death and Transformation, Pluto works both within the global field as well as within the personal field, undoing all that has been done, whilst retaining the knowledge that was born throughout past experiences. When the door is opened, you can't unsee what you have seen, so he finds a way, once the old has become obsolete, to transform your life in a big way for your highest good. When you cannot see the end or how things will work out, he can. He is emotionless yet slowly and confidently gets it (whatever your it is) done for your highest good. He does this even if the process is painful. We all tend to concentrate on the losses when things go wrong so tuning in to Pluto's frequency can help you feel more positive in difficult times.

These are the main planets and cosmic energies that have a major place within all of our energy centres. However, there are asteroids, which are considered planets, also influence, and play a similar role within our energy centres.

- **Ceres, Earth Mother:** Ceres is a dwarf planet, one of the four asteroid goddesses, which carries female issues into the social world and beyond. She is the cycle of the seasons and of lost innocence. She is motherly love and sacrifice. She is the nurturer and protector of humanity and represents the natural world. She is all about your relationship with the physical world because she is the harvest and your earth's star energy. She enables the connection between you and Gaia.

- **Chiron:** In addition to being the gardener of the soul, Chiron is a teacher and mentor. In essence, he is all about karmic release and understanding why we no longer need what we needed in the past. He is the teacher of letting go of what we have learned, gained, and achieved. He is about metaphysical matters. The bridge he represents binds together the body and consciousness, which is why he is also called 'the bridge.'

- **Poseidon:** It is Poseidon who awakens and reveals the truth. He is a magician as he reveals everything you need to know that wakes you up to what you need the most. Connection with the mystical, when it becomes real, opens your perception, and teaches you that the impossible is possible. Poseidon assist us in allowing, surrendering, and trusting that all you need to work with is energy.

FIRST ELEMENTAL LAW - ON THIS EMOTIONAL PLANE

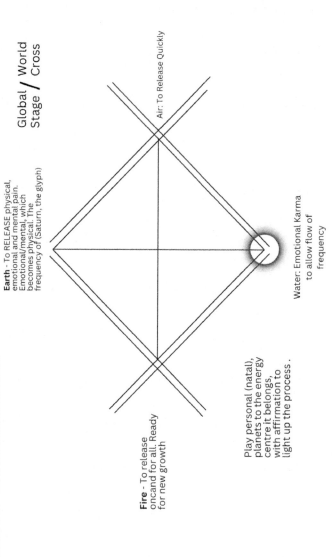

Global / World
Stage / Cross

Air: To Release Quickly

Earth - To RELEASE physical, emotional and mental pain. Emotional/mental, which becomes physical. The frequency of (Saturn, the glyph)

Water: Emotional Karma to allow flow of frequency

Play personal (natal), planets to the energy centre it belongs, with affirmation to light up the process .

Fire - To release oncand for all. Ready for new growth

This is the first elemental law on this plane, as you can see in the picture on the previous page. Using the cross in astrology, we represent our world stage, which is a cross from our global world stage to our personal world stage and our bodies using the energies of Mars, Moon, and Venus.

In the beginning, triangles are shown going down; then they go up in four strands indicating the phrase "as above, so below." Four is also the number of movements. As a result, the explanation of the conscious mind precedes the explanation of the unconscious mind.

Global stage of humans on the planet, where our brains resonate at 7.83 Hz, then below, where the planet resonates at 7.83 Hz, showing we are all connected by the same frequency if we wish to connect, which we do every millisecond unconsciously. Consciously connecting will bring synchronicity and flow state of creativity, as well as epiphanies and aha moments.

On the bottom of the cross, you can see the constellation of Cancer, the house of our beautiful moon, and the emotional reflection of our emotional intelligence.The beautiful moon , the planet, feeding her frequency daily as she makes her monthly reflective round of the planet earth.

Waxing Moon and ***Harvest*** are the keywords for this point, in conjunction with water, to flow around and through emotional issues that need our attention.

Then we follow up to the top where we have.

The constellation of the Oracle of the Dragon is Capricorn, also known as the house of our father energy which is Saturn who is physical energy and the teacher explaining that the root of all physical pain is emotion. This enables us to go within and find what we are learning through, the physical pain that we are enduring. We do this so we can move forward or as The Council puts it 'to undo all that has been done whilst retaining the knowledge'.

As we cross towards the right of this point, we come to the constellation of Love and Balance, which is the Ambassador that is Libra, the translator. Through Venus, the translator energy from the great central sun that passes through our sun which is then given to Mercury so we can link in through the element of Air. To connect with Venus, we need to understand the frequency she is passing on to our linear mind and resonate with it.

With air being a fast-acting energy, any planet or asteroid passing this point can use its energy. When the north wind blows, you can't ignore it. To achieve your emotional journey here on this planet, you need to find a balance between what stays and what goes. Keywords for this point are **_The Storyteller/ Defense._**

As you can see, this is an important journey, the first journey where we discover the tools within. Death does not exist, as they have shown, we just transition to another vibration in another form and go 'home', so to speak, to our soul family. Here, there is no judgment, just happiness. You can celebrate the fact that you have learned so much and The Council can look at what you have learned so you can first rest and then put your knowledge to use in another form, another dimension to another consciousness. As Neptune would say, 'there are limitless possibilities.'

So, my next step was attempting to put these in some kind of order.

The 12 Oracles

For the sovereignty of human consciousness, we channeled 360 meanings of each degree of the zodiac during the confinement in 2021.

How did we do this?

Over the preceding years I would unconsciously see decks of cards (in shops, on the internet, at fairs or given as gifts) and I would be really drawn to them. They would arrive home and on the shelf they would go. I was guided to collect as many sets of oracle cards and tarot decks as I could. Let me tell you, I'm not a card reader. I mean, I can but it doesn't give me joy, definitely not like Frequency Astrology does. So, I was confused but then one day they asked to get all the cards off the shelf. So, I did and then they went deck by deck and revealed it to be a star constellation.

Now I was interested!

Each day, they asked to meditate on a deck of cards, then shuffled them and one by one, they were chosen for each degree. After receiving a rune deck, it sat on the shelf with the cards, and then on the day the cards came out, I was given a constellation, and when the cards were shown, I was asked to blindly pick a rune for each card (since nothing is coincidence, it's synchronicity, my hand was guided, in a bag of runes), then it all came together.

Once we started using it in astrology, I was astounded by how clever we were. By 'we' I mean The Universe, The Field, Consciousness and The Solar System. It was the culmination of all the work we had been doing since 2012 that led to the birth of Frequency Astrology.

* * *

I awoke at 4AM on December 14th, 2020, with a kick of energy. I got out of bed and worked tirelessly until 9AM. What happened during this time is, all that what I had learned independently and what I had worked on in collaboration with The Council of Three consciously (and unconsciously) came together. By 9.15 that morning ***Frequency Astrology for New Awakening Consciousness*** was born.

In fact, even the name was channeled, and I felt so energized as it is the high frequency vibe that lifts you, as they say, love is the key.

Then, I was instructed to re-listen to my personal regression from 2018 (which was part of my training in Girona, Spain).

As I played it back, I heard that it wasn't just about my past lives on this planet but on other planets. The regression rebalanced that which needed to be rebalanced which was frequency and crystal energy. There was so much to take in. That I consciously had taken part in, everything over the past 8 years, but now I was going to write the 12 Oracles for you, the reader, to hear, read, and feel what you need to right now. For when you return to it again, and again, you will grow along with it and expand your perspective of yourself, your field, our beautiful world, her field, our solar system, and its field.

YOU CAN USE THIS TOOL TO MELD WITH OTHER TOOLS TO FLOW, THRIVE, LEARN, AND GROW AS A BEAUTIFUL AMAZING SOUL.

A Channeling:

> *Undo all that has been done whilst retaining the knowledge. This is the art of healing.*

> *I'm in deep water in Egypt in what is now called Sharm el- Sheikh...... open my eyes the sun is glittering through the sea I see a great turtle swim over me I see his shadow.*

> *As a being from a different planet, I came with many others to aid the humans. The pyramids act as gateways for entering the Pearl, which is the planet earth.*

> *I work in the great Sphinx. It is not now as*

you know it today. It was a great temple, what humans call great buildings that impart cosmic energy (which made us giggle, since you are the temple, you are the great building, and you are cosmic energy. It has rooms beneath. The great cosmic energy was imparted to gold by a great crystal. The gift would undo what had been done to them within their body as they wore it, letting them retain the knowledge that that gift had revealed.

As anything outside of a pyramid flourished, this place was very green and lush.

After getting out of the sea, I am energizing my 639 energies in my right hand and right foot. As I do so, I can feel heat or cold depending on which frequency I am generating. Connection energy is usually cold since we are connecting our inner and outer cosmos.

As I get out of the water, saltwater aids my frequency, and I work with other people who have long heads and are slim with long silky robes, all different colors. This is a very cosmopolitan place, where many races utilize a hub called Egypt, where we all live in harmony. My race generates frequency to assist any type of energy, including human energy. I impart the 639 to a group of humans sitting waiting, whose energy is weak, so they retain the knowledge, and as I do this, their energy is lifted, their vibration is lifted, so the gold jewelry we prepared in the Sphinx can aid in their undoing, and they will be of high (as you call it, we call it joy) frequency again.

I don't often do this, so it's fun. I work in the Sphinx and create frequency charts for all the races that come in from the cosmos (so they know which frequencies to use to aid them whilst on the Pearl). They come here for rest and to learn about emotion and to donate consciousness of their races to the Pearl as she is a great teacher and can impart this knowledge to whatever or whoever lives on or within her.

So, this aids this galaxy, your inner galaxy to flourish, then this aids all dimensions of cosmos and Universes it keeps energy moving.

I, as many have, chosen to incarnate in this time to bring back the knowledge your race once had, the joy of knowing, as you have forgotten, it has taken eons for this to happen, which is why when the sun shines on gold you feel happy, not the gold itself but what was once within it.

Healing keeps you in that space of in-perfectness since it is perfect in any state.

Undoing what has been done, while retaining knowledge, moves your energy beyond the dis-ease, into ease. Many teachers and leaders, who are here to empower those who have forgotten, are here on the Pearl, to enable the art of healing. As a result of the great conjunction in January 2020, you have experienced many changes. This is known as the shift, a cosmic shift of energy...which will be realized when the great eclipse on Dec 4th, 2021,then the great luna eclipse of May 5 th 2023 focuses all the energy within the pearls core and it becomes fully functioning, which is the undoing of what has been achieved.

When all your inner planets start moving forward, they are mirroring the outer planets, and your inner solar system will connect with the outer solar system (as it has always done unconsciously). Throughout the planet, there has been a new realization of dimensional frequency that has been occurring since the harmonic conversion of 1986 to 2012, which will allow magical things to occur if you allow them to.

You Are The Miracle

Start working with your inner solar system, start empowering yourself. Use your imagination, to enable the impossible.

Take advantage of your frequency to thrive, to release, to bring in this new energy - we've all been feeling the change - it's real, its quantum, it's an empowering time on the Pearl.

I send you love from the great turtle energy on the colour frequency of turquoise to enable the un-enabled, to empower the un-empowered and to enlighten those whose light has dimmed. To push forth those who are here to encourage all to vibrate on the love frequency for the highest good with gratitude and abundance.

We now have our energy centres and planets, and when we look at our astrology chart, we can start to locate them.

As I learned the language of astrology, it rapidly became apparent that it was much more than planets, asteroids, constellations, stars, and points in the solar system - it began much closer to home, inside, within each and every one of us.

As we are all one, through our fields collectively, so are all things. So, astrology was just a part of the story. We are now moving into a future timeline, for within this dimension, we are learning through the medium of time and space which is now our present, all things we do now we have already done.

The book has already been written, so we are just drawing from our future selves. We draw from a point of reference.

Why do we look up to the sky for inspiration?

Because we are looking at ourselves, but we just didn't have the key.

Astrology is one of the keys.

This is not as we have known it, but now with this new information, we can grow, push through, and connect to our future selves...

Is there a reason why all spiritual advisers, yogis, and monks say simply...Go within!

The hypnotherapy I used showed that we are all billions of years old, and we have lived many lives on many planets and in many solar systems. But this didn't feel enough, and I felt as if I needed more. Our first goal was to know what direct questions we needed to ask, so the past life regressionist could take us to a place where we could understand what was being revealed, so we needed a tool...

I had always had a head in the stars, loved astrology, but just played around with it. My dear friend Emma, who is an amazing psychic, suggested that I come to her for a reading. Despite knowing her for years, she had only given me one reading, when we first met.

So, I got in my car and drove up through the mountains to see her.

The reading was intense, fast, and different as there were two beings who came from another Universe to teach us about astrology. They wanted me to take a course in astrology and then forget everything I thought I knew. Then the learning would begin.

And it did.

During the course of three years, I channeled, not knowing what would take place, learning about frequencies, vibrations, mediation, spirit animals and dimensions.

The good news is that we can all channel as we are all portals. In fact, we need a channel to open the door and connect to our field. We can all do this in different ways, and this is the joy of learning.

Our company has grown rapidly since then, with clients who have charts and clients who have sessions. We have had amazing transformations, life changing experiences, tears of joy, amazement, understanding, a sense of being fed when we take your personal frequency, lay you down on a session bed, and play to your energy centres. Through amazing lessons, some are aided. Our plan is to teach those who wish to become frequency practitioners, in the near future, to write the book first, so all can be vibrationally aided with this tool.

So, let's put it all together.

We have provided you with a list of the personal frequencies that you can use to connect with the collective frequencies of consciousness and ask the questions you need. A personal frequency is the frequency for the field that you brought with you, the exact time when you were born, the exact date and place where you were born (if you don't know the exact time, we use an average of 12 hours). Make your chart by using frequency astrology. It can be made and sent to you with a full explanation at dragonseyehub.com.

Once you have your chart of your personal frequencies, then you can connect to your own conscious frequencies, your field, go within and ask personal questions, personal to you, and get personal answers, to understand yourself more consciously, by going on a conscious journey.

Remember we talked as if you were your mobile phone, then you could connect to your own conscious frequencies, your field, go within and ask personal questions, personal to you, and get personal answers, in order to understand yourself more consciously, by going on a conscious journey So let's look at your stomach for instance on the right you have mercury the conscious mind, on the left you have the moon, if the feeling is all over the stomach area, We know it is to do with emotional intelligence (moon)coming in to your conscious mind.

Since we know where the feeling or pain is coming from, we can use our frequency...our personal moon frequency. If you want to find the frequency, simply visit dragonseyehub.com and click on the orange button that says frequency directory. Press it, and you will see all the frequencies we use right now. Simply click on the frequency and play it, for a minute, ten minutes, or an hour.

Below is the frequency directory explained.

In this frequency directory, you may find information that we have already covered, but we felt it needed to be included in its entirety.

Frequency directory

Taken from dragonseyehub.com (the home of frequency astrology) where you will find all the frequencies with explanations are here for your evolving body, mind, and spirit. Just click and play.

The collective frequencies are below. They are to be used as a guide. Please visit the Dragon's Eye Hub Blog for more information.

The frequencies will assist you in thriving through this evolutionary time, and they will enable you to thrive with ease. These frequencies are for the evolving body, so they are in different energy centres than those of the norm.

Astrological Personal Frequency Chart

You can take a more personal journey by creating your own frequency chart. As discussed previously, you will have specific frequencies for specific energy centres that you brought with you at the exact time, date and place you were born.

Your personal chart will enable you to see how your personal energy centres (chakras), are best tuned in too. The following is a list of the collective, the factory setting of the human energy field. After you have your chart made, you will be able to tune into your own frequency. For instance, if you are about to have a conversation, or a meeting, you might want to play your personal frequency of your throat energy centre.

How do they work?

You can find an explanation of the field at the bottom of this directory. All energy centres are connected to the surrounding organs and skin of the body.

You will feel a sensation or pain when the emotional body within your field is trying to communicate that there is a feeling that needs to be released, and you are unaware of it. You may also be releasing some past life issue or collective karma.

It is best to start with intention, in order to restore ease to the body from dis-ease. Louise Hays' book, You Can Heal Your Life, contains a set of affirmations along with an emotional probable cause to get you started. Play the frequency while saying the affirmation four times, then see what happens. You can also just play the frequency with the intention of creating ease within the body. Play them around the house or at night whilst sleeping.

In fact, as I'm writing this, I'm playing a frequency.

Astrology, that was shown to me as a language. Upon learning the language, it became apparent very quickly that astrology wasn't just about planets, asteroids, constellations, stars, and points outside the solar system, but began much closer to home, inside each of us.

* * *

- **For pain, 174 Hz, Earth energy (masculine)**: Saturating your field with 174 HZ will show you how your physical body reacts, giving you some peace. If you can put your bare feet or hands on earth and play your earth star centre, this would have a great effect on your personal pain. Earth Star energy centre, place of release .Through your hands and feet ,the place of balance .

- **For Earth Energy, 285 Hz (feminine):** Play this for balance of the two energies, for your energy and equilibrium. The lower root is ruled by Venus, and by Mars.

- **For inflammation, 136.10 HZ**

- **For Transformation, 111 Hz** will also help with inflammation, see which one is best for you.

- **For Communication, 396 Hz:** Root energy centre, expansion of foundation, good for grounding.

- **For Emotional Intelligence, 417 Hz:** Sacral energy centre is the home of the sun energy centre. Galactic messages are sent through this energy centre.

- **For Love Frequency, 528 Hz:** This is the energy centre, where emotional messages come through, where the conscious mind rules and the emotional mind follows, this is where you feel what the messages are.

- **For Healing, 639 Hz:** Higher healing truth, your limitless receiver way out in the cosmos.

- **For Balance, 741 Hz:** Transformation through speech. This is where change takes place.

- **For Eye Energy, 852 Hz:** In the third eye energy centre you will see liberation through disciplined thought. Saturn your dragon lives here, if your mind is in an alpha state, you can bring in whatever you need. Within the new synapses in the brain, Uranus creates new roads for your dragon to manifest.

- **For Connection, 963 Hz:** Liberation, revolution through disciplined thought, where thought is replaced by feeling, connection.

- **For Universe Energy, 432 Hz:** The frequency of our beautiful Universe.

- **For Shekina Energy, 1185 Hz:** The frequency of sacred knowledge through your DNA.

* * *

The frequency directory is available in full on the website, and you can play the frequency by clicking on the link below each frequency (or search for online videos by putting in the frequency you need to listen to). When you do this, sit quietly, and see what comes to you.

You will know a message is coming either by smell, vision or synchronicity which will come into your field physically. This may be a song on the radio, or simply a comment somebody says that suddenly has deeper meaning to me. Once you start to use it, it will amplify with other methods of connecting.

Now, let's talk about frequencies and vibrations and how they work within your energy centres. Once you start to play the frequency and begin to feel where it speaks to you, you will start to connect to the Universe and your higher self. It is here, in your soul, that you start to create with your field.

Suddenly, things around you become messages and the more you play with this, the more you will start to understand the language that is being used for communication.

For example, I was once shown a book of numbers and now, I receive messages through numbers very often. I use my book to look up the message. Another example. When I'm about to speak with a client, I play my throat energy centre frequency, which will allow me to connect to what

I need to say. If you play the frequency of the throat energy centre of the person you are speaking to, they will be able to speak up, and join in on the conversation. Play the collective frequency of the throat energy centre for collective speech or talk, so everyone can gain what they need from this experience.

During a seminar, for instance, the collective throat energy centre will work well. It is possible to play the collective healing frequency of 639 hz in a doctor's surgery or hospital. Or you can play the collective frequency of the earth star, 174 hz, which releases pain, or the ohm frequency, which releases inflammation.

There is no right or wrong, there just is. Play what you feel you are guided to play for the given situation you are in.

Why the solfeggio frequencies?

Solfeggio frequencies have been used since ancient times for a reason. They are the frequencies that connect you to the Universe. The original sacred notes were used in the Gregorian chant "Ut Queant Laxis (Hymn To St. John, The Baptist). Known as one or the most inspirational hymns ever written and features the original 6 solfeggio notes. As the solfeggio notes combine, they penetrate deeply into the subconscious mind, then into the conscious mind, promoting healing and transformation.

In the 11th century, a Benedictine monk named the 6 notes of the hexachord after the first syllable of each line of the Latin hymn to St John the Baptist. In addition to the base solfeggio frequency, we now work with many other frequencies, which carry the solfeggio frequency with action. As we evolve, so will the vibrations, frequencies, so more will come into play.

And this is just the start!

How exciting.

Chapter 5
Affirmations

Let's talk about affirmations and how they are able to electrify our entire system.

A picture of the human form is shown on the next page, along with affirmations.

These are the 'root' affirmations, the sort of affirmations we use as a starting point.

They then lead to personal affirmations. There are more affirmations for the practitioner to guide you with when you are in session. We are also working on a deck of cards that you can use along with your frequency.

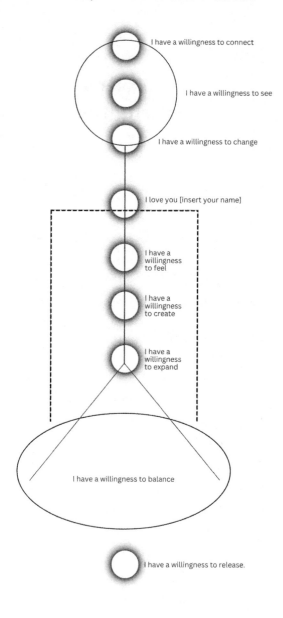

You can use affirmations to deprogram your mind and guide your inner narrative. They are a guidance system that allows your field (and your entire body) to know what your intention is. They also serve as a message provider that reveals the truth your body is trying to communicate.

You can use affirmations to undo a subconscious process you wish to change.

Whenever you feel a niggle, such as a sore throat, look to the affirmation, you can see that this energy centre is about change, the sore throat is a resistance to change.

In saying an affirmation (out loud or in your head), you are guiding your physical, emotional, and mental bodies. This allows your sovereignty, you are guiding, you are putting your foot in the door with the word willingness. Thus, allowing the process you are going through, the resistance to know it is no longer needed.

My work has shown me over the years how pain starts as a niggle, but if you ignore it, it will grow as it is a message from your emotional body.

These affirmations serve as a guide for your field's action, and pain or accidents are often reactions to the message, a form of resistance, either consciously or unconsciously.

When you have a long-standing problem, it is often hard for you to let go of the resistance, as it becomes part of you. In addition to aiding, you and others in learning, longstanding pain (or dis-ease) can also assist you in opening your perspective of compassion, allowing different actions to be taken and reactions to be observed, which may lead you to be healed.

As you co-create everything within your field, the body hears everything. Eventually, you may create a longstanding dis-ease of the body that perhaps will take longer to release because it took you a long time to create. However, an exception to this is when you hear of 'miracle' cures that occur when a person is truly ready to release what has been concerning them emotionally.

A great tool for this is Forgiveness.

All I have consciously learned from this work is that physical pain is the fruit of emotional and mental pain. To undo the physical, you must undo the emotional and mental as well. That is why affirmations are effective.

I would now like to share the personal experience of affirmation with you and how they shape my everyday life.

The Alchemy of Affirmation & Intention

Affirmations aid us through the changing energies of the paradigm we are traveling through.

As I shared previously, in 2012 I was spiritually awokenand aided by my friend Emma when she and her husband came to visit our BnB in the south of France.

Just a few years later, in 2014, I had dislocated 3 discs in my lower back. I was looking at an operation and I was bed bound with a visiting nurse twice per day to inject me with huge doses of anti-inflammatory drugs. My femoral artery was not getting the blood supply it needed and I had lost 28 lbs. in just over one month.

As the doctors and nurses continued to work on my body, I decided to work on my body too. While they dealt with the physical side of things, I worked on the spiritual side using affirmations continuously.

And it worked.

The combination of physical and spiritual, this healed and aided the slipped discs in my back to go back into place. Suddenly, the doctor stopped talking about how I would be on pain killers for the rest of my life and eventually get arthritis. Instead, I was simply free to heal, and my body could restore itself to naturally good health. I then started working with a physiotherapist who was equally amazed at my quick recovery. She wanted to know what incredible pain killers I must be taking as I was walking as if there had never been anything wrong with my back, even in heels.

I didn't say anything at the moment. Instead, I picked up my copy of Louise Hay's You Can Heal Your Life and showed it to her. Then, I said, 'I've been reprogramming myself through affirmations by bringing attention to what has been concealed and in need of my attention'.

On some level, I expected her to criticize the use of affirmations, but her response astonished me.

She looked me dead in the eyes and said, 'If all my clients used that book, then I would be out of a job'.

Skipping forward to 2018, I had decided to learn regression hypnotherapy and a friend and I took a journey together to complete a BQH training program. In this training we learned the power of intention and how if we focus enough from our heart to our mind then we can achieve almost everything.

She demonstrated this through a simple practice.

The Glass of Water Practice

Get a glass of water.

Take a drink.

Observe how it tastes.

Then place the glass on the palm of your hand.

Imagine a bright white light hovering over the top of your head.

Then envision filling the white light with the intention of love that is coming directly from your heart.

Imagine that same white light traveling through your body and down the arm that is holding the glass of water.

Visualize the light entering the glass and swirling within the water.

Now, take a drink.

My experience of this exercise was that the water tasted completely differently the second time around. Almost as if it had been infused with roses.

In that moment, I consciously knew about intention and how you can put intention into any part of your life.

Many people may be familiar with the work of Dr. Emote and his experiences with water. They were made famous in the documentary *What the Bleep Do We Know* and highlighted how verbally directing different messages to glasses of water affected how the particles crystallized. If you're not aware of his work, then I advise you to get on the internet right now and watch some videos about his astonishing findings.

With this in mind, you can now begin to contemplate that you can control your own body with your higher self as the body listens to what you tell it. For example, when someone says to me, "don't come near me or you'll catch my cold", I tell myself (and them), 'don't worry, I won't catch your cold'.

Another affirmation for health I use three to four times a day is.

Thank you for keeping all my bodies in complete harmony and optimum physical emotional and mental health, for my highest good always, and so it is,so it is, and so it is.As I'm doing this I'm feeling it from my heart ....

Go on, try it.

In this energetic shifting time, we can steer our body like a true admiral of the fleet.

In the beginning, I wrote the affirmations on a piece of paper and placed them in my handbag, in the bathroom, by my bed, until I knew them all. They changed my inner programming, they changed my inner narrative, which changed my outer world. I was able to take my brace off that I had to wear to support my back, and I did not need the tablets, as the pain was descending. It stopped hurting one day when I got out of bed.

When I went shopping with friends, I used the affirmation to find a bag I really liked. Without asking how much it cost, I just took it off the shelves, walked up to the assistant, and confidently said, 'I'm taking it'. My friend asked me how much it would cost, and I told her that I didn't need to know since everything I needed was already covered. It turned out that I had the exact amount of money in my purse for the handbag. The Universe was supporting me. I know something like a bag sounds trivial but it's another powerful example.

The feeling of not having enough exists in all of us, but we are abundantly amazing creatures and can find a better feeling within ourselves through affirmations.

For example, the first question I ask someone with back problems is, *'How do you feel about money?'*

Why?

Because I believe lower back problems are correlated with a feeling of lack.

And how can we reprogram this?

With affirmations because they guide the inner narrative.

However, if you want to increase the power of affirmation then I suggest using them with the frequencies because the changes will occur much more rapidly since the frequency is quantum.

Through vibration, which is another word for frequency, the elegant magnetics get to work within the space around the cells. A message may come to you if you're not ready for release, such as a cold or chest infection, where you are resisting change, not loving the self that is you, not taking life in, feeling the negativity of the collective...these are all messages.

Perhaps, before it gets physical, we can be honest with ourselves, forgive ourselves and others, and then start to love ourselves.

We take a little exercise that we enjoy, whatever our field needs, play your personal frequencies that light it up with affirmations.

I play frequency daily, playing all my energy centres, then starting with affirmations if I feel a niggle.

Say your affirmation at least four times a day, it's not as hard as you think, it's quick, and takes only seconds. I still use mine for my back, my throat, and for all my energy centres, because we are all on a journey.

With these techniques you can train your body through the field if you get physical signs or dis-ease.

You can use frequency with medication, herbal remedies, playing while doing yoga, walking, running, whatever you are guided to do.

One way to find what you need is to go within.

This is only the beginning, what you do with it is up to you.

This is YOUR journey.

When affirmation, which is intention, is said using frequency, it becomes quantum.

Let's talk Oracles, which ties all of this together, including a definition of each degree.

A Channeling

A personal awakening...

The magic of unity, how we amplify together...Sarah in Barbados, Matthew in Hawaii....put hands on your heart energy centre, then open all your energy centres, there stands a gate ...the great gathering ...here is where you will meet others if you allow, here is where you will discover others.

Chapter 6
The 12 Oracles

The 12 oracles are one of the ways that we can comprehend how the Universe communicates with us through the outer solar system within the limitations of our three-dimensional linear brain. Furthermore, they subsequently explain how this then connects to our inner solar system.Let's start the conversation with the fact that The Astrology Wheel is divided up into 12 sectors as follows;

The first quadrant is made up of *Oracles 1 ,2, 3.*

The second quadrant is made up of *Oracles 4, 5, 6.*

The third quadrant is made up of *Oracles 7, 8, 9.*

The fourth quadrant is made up of *Oracles 10, 11, 12.*

. . .

These oracles Work on a gaiacentric perspective, a.k.a an earthly perspective. In other words, frequency astrology is Gaia-centric, meaning it is consciousness centred from the consciousness of this earth.

There are 12 oracles each with 30 of their own keywords. On the list of key points, to keep it simple, this is the abridged version.The full version will be within the astrologer's book, the next book to come out.

You can use the planet position on your natal chart to find your specific keywords to help you expand during your lifetime.

To keep things simple, each oracle holds these key points;

• Star system (E.g. Aries or Capricorn)

• Frequency of the particular star system

So, how does it work?

When a planet, point or asteroid is passing by to a certain degree, play the frequency of an oracle and sit quietly and see what comes through for you. Use this information simply as a starting point.

There are two definitions for each degree. For example, 91 degrees is The Full Moon and The Gateway. Meditating on both definitions of a certain degree simply gives you a starting point to see what comes through for you.

How to put this into practice

1. First identify the planet you want to work with (maybe your sun).
2. On the natal chart, find the star sign and degree.
3. Scroll down the oracles and find the star constellation (star sign), then scroll down and find the keyword by finding the number of degree of your planet and across from the degree number is your *key* word.
4. Play the frequency of the star constellation whilst sitting with the keywords and see what comes up for you.
5. Maybe the keywords mean something to you already but were unconscious of.

Aries

Here on earth, this is the male divine energy that provides you with the energetic push necessary to get things moving.

STAR SYSTEM: ARIES

FREQUENCY: 174 HZ(MALE)

00°.00'. JOURNEY OPENING ACTIVATION

DEFINITION 1   **DEFINITION 2**

00°
CONSCIOUSNESS   POSSESSIONS

01°
MIRACLE   GROWTH

02°
THROAT ENERGY CENTRE   WARRIOR

03°
COHERENCE   GATEWAY

04°
ROOT ENERGY CENTRE   OPENING

05°
COSMIC FLOWER   JOY

06°
PROSPERITY   OPENING

07°
INTEGRATION   DISRUPTION

08°
DISCERNMENT   FLOW

09°
ALCHEMY.   WARRIOR

10°
REMEMBRANCE.   DISRUPTION

11°
PASSION.   GROWTH

12°
GAIA   CONSTRAINT

13°
TANTRIC JOURNEY.   GROWTH

14°
MERKABAH.   OPENING

15°
TRANSITION.   INITIATION

16°
COMMUNICATION.   STANDSTILL

17°
SACRAL ENERGY CENTRE.   INITIATION

18°
EARTH.   FLOW

19°
CONCEPTION.   INITIATION

20°
HEALING.   SEPARATION

21°
EMERGENCE.   DEFENCE

22°
DELIGHT.   UNKNOWABLE

23°
SOUL TIME.   OPENING

24°
COMPASSION.   WARRIOR

25°
DIVINE MASCULINE.   OPENING

26°
BELIEF.   MOVEMENT

27°
REALISATION.   WHOLENESS

28°
UNIVERSAL LOVE.   INITIATION

29°
HEART ENERGY CENTRE.   FERTILITY

Taurus

STAR SYSTEM: *CONSTELLATION OF TAURUS*

FREQUENCY: 285 Hz (F)

MEANING OF EACH DEGREE

30°00'
HATHOR GATEWAY
HAWK........EARTH ....CONSTRAINT

1°
BEAR..........EARTH..........POSSESSIONS

2°
MOTH.......AIR....................STANDSTILL

3°
OWL..........AIR....................GROWTH

4°
BEAVER....WATER.............WHOLENESS

5°
WHALE.....WATER.............SEPARATION

6°

OYSTER....WATER.............FLOW

7°

DRAGONFLY...AIR............GROWTH

8°

PHOENIX.........SPIRIT........BREAKTHROUGH

9°

COBRA.............FIRE...........OPENING

10°

ZEBRA............FIRE.............CONSTRAINT

11°

FISH................WATER........THE SELF

12°

PEACOCK......AIR...............UNKNOWABLE

13°

FIREFLY..........AIR................BREAKTHROUGH

14°

ELK................EARTH..........DISRUPTION

15°

BEE...............AIR.................OPENING

16°
FROG............WATER............INITIATION

17°
UNICORN....SPIRIT.............DÉFENSE

18°
BUTTERFLY...AIR...............FERTILITY

19°
BAT..................AIR............UNKNOWABLE

20°
MOUSE...........EARTH......JOURNEY

21°
CROW.............AIR.............PROTECTION

22°
SPIDER...........EARTH.......GATEWAY

23°
LIZARD...........FIRE............POSSESSIONS

24°
PANTHER......FIRE............FERTILITY

25°
EAGLE............AIR................HARVEST

26°
TURTLE..........WATER.........DÉFENSE

27°
CHEETAH......FIRE..............GATEWAY

28°
BUFFALO.......EARTH..........GATEWAY

29°
ELEPHANT.....FIRE................STANDSTILL

Gemini

STAR SYSTEM: *CONSTELLATION OF GEMINI*

FREQUENCY: 396 HZ

MEANING OF EACH DEGREE

00°
4 OF EARTH ....UNKNOWABLE

1°
21 WORLD -PERSPECTIVE.......DISRUPTION

2°
14 PATIENCE.......................................WHOLENESS

3°
10 FORTUNES WHEEL.....................WARRIOR
Destiny meets synchronicity

4°
10 OF WATER.................................SIGNALS

5°
12 HANGED MAN ....BALANCE

6°
19 SUN...PROTECTION

7°
16 TOWER..WHOLENESS

8°
7 OF EARTH.....................................POSSESSIONS

9°
10 OF FIRE..SIGNALS

10°
ACE OF EARTH................................OPENING

11°
7 OF FIRE...SIGNALS

12°
7 CHARIOT...FLOW

13°
PAGE OF AIR.....................................DEFENSE

14°
KING OF AIR.....................................WHOLENESS

15°
MESSENGER OF WATER.............OPENING

16°
KING OF WATER............................WHOLENESS

17°
3 OF FIRE..PROTECTION

18°
3 OF WATER.....................................GROWTH

19°
9 OF EARTH.....................................PARTNERSHIP

20°
9 OF AIR..SIGNALS

21°
18 MOON..JOURNEY

22°
9 HERMIT..WARRIOR

23°
13 TRANSFORMATIONS.............UNKNOWABLE

24°
4 EMPEROR.....................................PROTECTION

24°
4 EMPEROR.....................................PROTECTION

25°
9 OF AIR...STANDSTILL

26°
MESSENGER OF AIR......................BREAKTHROUGH

27°
PAGE OF FIRE.................................WARRIOR

28°
7 OF AIR...BREAKTHROUGH

29°
8 OF WATER....................................STANDSTILL

Cancer

STAR SYSTEM: *CONSTELLATION OF CANCER*

FREQUENCY: 417 HZ

MEANING OF EACH DEGREE

00°
WAXING MOON ....HARVEST

1°
FULL MOON ♉ ....GATEWAY

2°
MUTABLE MOON..................DISRUPTION

3°
NEW MOON ♉ ....WARRIOR

4°
VOID-OF COURSE-MOON.......SIGNALS

5°
FULL MOON ♏ ....UNKNOWABLE

6°
FULL MOON ♈ ....UNKNOWABLE

7°
NORTH NODE...........................FLOW

8°
NEW MOON ECLIPSE...............JOURNEY

9°
GIBBOUS MOON........................HARVEST

10°
SOUTH NODE...........................FLOW

11°
NEW MOON ♍...........................GATEWAY

12°
NEW MOON ♓...........................INITIATION

13°
FULL MOON ♒........................FERTILITY

14°
WANING MOON ....HARVEST

15°
NEW MOON ♑ ....GROWTH

16°
FULL MOON ♌ ....FLOW

17°
NEW MOON ♌ ....PROTECTION

18°
HOLD YOUR VISION..................BREAKTHROUGH

19°
NEW MOON ♎ ....DEFENSE

20°
BALSAMIC MOON ....FERTILITY

21°
FULL MOON ♓ .........................BREAKTHROUGH

22°
FULL MOON...............................DEFENSE

23°
FULL MOON♋ ....SEPARATION

24°
FULL MOON ♐ ....WHOLENESS

25°
FULL MOON ♎ ....WARRIOR

26°
NEW MOON ♐ ....HARVEST

27°
FULL MOON ECLIPSE.................GROWTH

28°
NEW MOON ♋ ....CONSTRAINT

29°
NEW MOON ....INITIATION

Leo

STAR SYSTEM: *CONSTELLATION OF LEO*

FREQUENCY: 528 HZ

MEANING OF EACH DEGREE

0°
SCYTHE .... GROWTH

1°
MAN .... PROTECTION

2°
LETTER .... THE SELF

3°
HEART .... UNKNOWABLE

4°
COFFIN ....MOVEMENT

5°
TREE .... DISRUPTION

6°
BOOK .... BALANCE

7°
OWL-BIRD .... INITIATION

8°
CLOUDS .... DEFENSE

9°
HOUSE .... WHOLENESS

10°
CHILD .... WARRIOR

11°
SNAKE .... PARTNERSHIP

12°
STORK .... HARVEST

13°
RIDER .... BREAKTHROUGH

14°
CROSS .... HARVEST

15°
FLOWERS ....DEFENCE

16°
FISH .... FERTILITY

17°
BEAR ....JOURNEY

18°
ANCHOR .... INITIATION

19°
DOG .... THE SELF

20°
SUN .... HARVEST

21°
MOUSE .... PARTNERSHIP

22°
TOWER .... UNKNOWABLE

23°
STAR .... HARVEST

24°
MOUNTAIN .... CONSTRAINT

25°
LILY .... STRENGTH

26°
GARDEN .... INITIATION

27°
WHIP .... BREAKTHROUGH

28°
WOMAN .... HARVEST

29°
MOON .... DEFENSE

Virgo

STAR SYSTEM: *CONSTELLATION OF VIRGO*

FREQUENCY: 639 HZ

MEANING OF EACH DEGREE

0°
NUMBER 27 .... SILVER .... WHOLENESS

1°
NUMBER 9 ....CHERRY ....GATEWAY

2°
NUMBER 15 ....AMBER ....THE SELF

3°
NUMBER 1 ....RAINBOW .... UNKNOWABLE

4°
NUMBER 13 ....CHOCOLATE ....GATEWAY

5°
NUMBER 28 .... BLACK .... OPENING

6°

NUMBER 42 .... LILAC ....GATEWAY

7°

NUMBER 24 .... WHITE .... UNKNOWABLE

8°

NUMBER 8 .... RUBY .... THE SELF

9°

NUMBER 29 ....GREY ....CONSTRAINT

10°

NUMBER 16 ....ORANGE ....FERTILITY

11°

NUMBER 11 .... AUBURN .... STANDSTILL

12°

NUMBER 45 ....VIOLET ....INITIATION

13°

NUMBER 43 .... MAUVE ....JOY

14°

NUMBER 44 .... LAVENDER .... UNKNOWABLE

15°

NUMBER 2 .... RED .... JOURNEY

16°

NUMBER 33 .... AQUA ....GATEWAY

17°

NUMBER 4 ....PINK ....PARTNERSHIP

18°

NUMBER 35 .... CYAN ....HARVEST

19°

NUMBER 38 .... SAPPHIRE .... JOURNEY

20°

NUMBER 34 .... TURQUOISE ....SEPARATION

21°

NUMBER 17 .... TANGERINE .... SIGNALS

22°

NUMBER 40 ....INDIGO ....WARRIOR

23°

NUMBER 37 ....BLUE .... STRENGTH

24°

NUMBER 32 .... JADE ....SEPARATION

25°

NUMBER18 .... CORAL ....INITIATION

26°
NUMBER 30 .... EMERALD ....BALANCE

27°
NUMBER 10 .... BURGUNDY ....WARRIOR

28°
NUMBER 39 ....PURPLE .... GROWTH

29°
NUMBER 41 ....PLUM ....FLOW

Oracle Seven

Libre

STAR SYSTEM: *CONSTELLATION OF LIBRE*

FREQUENCY: 741 HZ

MEANING OF EACH DEGREE

0°
THE STORY TELLER .... DEFENSE

1°
A HIGHER VIEW ....UNKNOWABLE

2°
A MERRY MOTIVE .... SIGNALS

3°
NUMBER 26 .... GREAT BIG LOVE ....DEFENSE

4°
NUMBER 45 ...BEYOND THE ORDINARY...FERTILITY

5°

NUMBER 48 ...A BURST OF MAGIC ...POSSESSIONS

6°

NUMBER 30 ... SHINING THROUGH ... SIGNALS

7°

NUMBER 9 ... THE ROSES KIS ... PROTECTION

8°

NUMBER 16 ....THE ROYAL YOU ... STRENGTH

9°

NUMBER 49 ...WILLING RELEASE ... GROWTH

10°

NUMBER 44 ... DIVINE MATRIX ... POSSESSIONS

11°

NUMBER 27 ... A GRAND SYMPHONY ... INITIATION

12°

NUMBER 31 ... CALL OF THE MUSE ... MOVEMENT

13°

NUMBER 2 ... RODS OF ABUNDANCE ...DISRUPTION

14°

NUMBER 3 ... TIME MACHINE ... PROTECTION

15°

NUMBER 36 ... SEEING BEYOND ... BREAKTHROUGH

16°

NUMBER 6 ... IT IS WHAT IT IS ... OPENING

17°

NUMBER 42 ... SMOKE AND MIRRORS ... POSSESSIONS

18°

NUMBER 47 ... SACRED REVERENCE ... CONSTRAINT

19°

NUMBER 34 ... OPENING TO DISCOVERY ... WHOLENESS

20°

NUMBER 35 ... A TALL TALE ... MOVEMENT

21°

NUMBER 19 ... WALKING THE LION ... STANDSTILL

22°

NUMBER 24 ... LET IT GO ... CONSTRAINT

23°

NUMBER 46 ... THE UNCHARTED SEA ... DISRUPTION

24°

NUMBER 4 ... GREAT AND FULL ... GATEWAY

25°

NUMBER 23 ... HEALING THE HEART ... JOY

26°

NUMBER 25 ... BIRDS OF A FEATHER ... THE SELF

27°

NUMBER 11 ... IN PERFECT HARMONY ... STANDSTILL

28°

NUMBER 18 ... THE POWER OF PURPOSE ... FERTILITY

29°

NUMBER 22 ... TENDER EMBRACE ... GATEWAY

Scorpio

STAR SYSTEM: *CONSTELLATION OF SCORPIO*

FREQUENCY: 852 HZ

MEANING OF EACH DEGREE

0°
NUMBER 44 ....PROTECTION...........STANDSTILL

1°
NUMBER 18 ....TETRAHEDRON ....FERTILITY

2°
NUMBER 27 ....528 HZ ....PARTNERSHIP

3°
NUMBER 0 ....AWAKENING ....SIGNALS

4°
NUMBER 21 ... ICOSAHEDRON (FEMININE DIVINE) ... MOVEMENT

5°
NUMBER 35 ....EXPANSION ....GATEWAY

6°

NUMBER 28 ....639 HZ ....THE SELF

7°

NUMBER 47 ....VITALITY ....DEFENCE

8°

NUMBER 41 ....INNER CHILD ....CONSTRAINT

9°

NUMBER 42 ....JOY ....SEPARATION

10°

NUMBER 45 ....REFLECTION ....HARVEST

11°

NUMBER 10 ... UNLIMITED POTENTIAL ... BALANCE

12°

NUMBER 3 ....LOVE FREQUENCY ....OPENING

13°

NUMBER 6 ....RAVEN MAGIK ....FERTILITY

14°

NUMBER 23 ....174 HZ ............BREAKTHROUGH

15°

NUMBER 36 ....FOUNDATION..........MOVEMENT

18°

NUMBER 14 ... FRUIT OF LIFE (SPHERES OF KNOWLEDGE) ... OPENING

19°

NUMBER 22 ... DODECAHEDRON ... BREAKTHROUGH

20°

NUMBER 15 ... METATRON CUBE ... BALANCE

21°

NUMBER 43 ... MEDITATION ... GATEWAY

22°

NUMBER 46 ... SURRENDER ... SEPARATION

23°

NUMBER 33 ... BELIEVE ... PARTNERSHIP

24°

NUMBER 34 ... CLARITY ... THE SELF

25°

NUMBER 04 ... MERKABAH HEALING ... THE SELF

26°

NUMBER 31 ... 963 HZ ... GATEWAY

27°

NUMBER 13 ... FLOWER OF LIFE ... DEFENCE

28°
NUMBER 29 ....741 HZ ....SEPARATION

29°
NUMBER 25 ... 396 HZ (RELEASE FROM GUILT AND FEAR) ....OPENING

SAGITTARIUS
PART 1

We are dealing within an oracle within an oracle, so there will be 2 x the meaning for some degrees.

STAR SYSTEM: CONSTELLATION OF SAGITTARIUS WORKING WITH THE PLEIADES.

FREQUENCY: 963 HZ

MEANING OF EACH DEGREE

0°
MERCURY ............BREAKTHROUGH

1°
DJWAL KHUL .... SIGNALS

2°
ODIN ....WARRIOR

3°
MAHAVATAR BABAJI ....SEPERATION

4°
MASTER BUDDAH ....OPENING

5°
HILARION ....JOY

6°
RADHA .... BREAKTHROUGH

7°
HORUS ....FERTILITY

8°
SANAT KUMARA............STRENGTH

9°
MARY MAGDALENE ....WHOLENESS

10°
SAINT GERMAIN ....FLOW

11°
SERAPIS BEY .... INITIATION

12°
BRIGID ....CONSTRAINT

13°
ARCHANGEL MICHEAL ....GROWTH

14°
THE MYRIAM ....JOY

15°
ISIS ....OPENING

16°
JOAN OF ARC ....GROWTH

17°
EL MORYA ....GATEWAY

18°
GAIA ....WHOLENESS

19°
HOPE ....FLOW

20°
LORD GANESH ....WARRIOR

21°
MOTHER MARY ....DISRUPTION

22°
HOLY AMETHYST ....HARVEST

23°
GREEN TARA ....JOY

24°
CHARITY ....POSSESSIONS

25°
LADY PORTIA ....UNKNOWABLE

26°
LADY VENUS ....JOY

27°
FREYA ....POSSESSIONS

28°
THE SHEKINAH ....WARRIOR

29°
CERUNNOS............CONSTRAINT

SAGITTARIUS
PART 2 / OPHIUCHUS

The snake and the fire conjoin with the human, the Kundalini of humanity.

To enable a deeper picture of your own DNA, we have an extra spark of light to assist you in shining your light.

Playing the frequency of 963 HZ and working with the definitions laid out will assist you in building a clear picture of your own personal journey.

MEANING OF EACH DEGREE

7°
YOUR LIFE IS A CANVAS ....PARTNERSHIP

8°
FORGE, DON'T FOLLOW ....GROWTH

9°
CHILD OF THE COSMOS ....THE SELF

10°
INNER EARTH ....WARRIOR

11°
STAR KEEPER ....BALANCE

12°
STAR BATHING ....MOVEMENT

13°
ALL PATHS LEAD HOME ....UNKNOWABLE

14°
YOU GOT THE LOVE ....SEPARATION

15°
KARMIC RELATIONSHIPS ....DISRUPTION

16°
MESSENGER ....WARRIOR

17°
JUMP-IN ....MOVEMENT

18°
EARTH SCHOOL ....STRENGTH

19°
PERSPECTIVE .... THE SELF

20°
EARTH PULSING ....SEPERATION

21°
STAR BROTHERS ....WHOLENESS

22°
THE VOID ....GROWTH

23°
FACE YOUR TRUE NORTH, YOU ARE NOT FOR
EVERYONE ....FERTILITY

24°
IM SORRY .... MOVEMENT

25 °
EMPATHIC STAR SEED ....STRENGTH

Oracle Ten

CAPRICORN

STAR SYSTEM: *THE CONSTELLATION THAT IS CAPRICORN, THE ANDROMEDAS*

FREQUENCY: 111 HZ

MEANING OF EACH DEGREE

0°
DARK BLUE GALACTIC DRAGON ....DISRUPTION

1°
DEEP BLUE DRAGON ....SIGNALS

2°
EARTH AND FIRE DRAGON ....WHOLENESS

3°
GOLDEN SOLAR DRAGON ....CONSTRAINT

4°
ROYAL BLUE AND GOLD DRAGON ....INITIATION

5°
AIR DRAGON ....GATEWAY

6°

ROSE PINK DRAGON ....STANDSTILL

7°

WATER DRAGON ....SIGNALS

8°

FIRE DRAGON ....OPENING

9°

LILAC FIRE DRAGON .... HARVEST

10°

ARCHANGEL GABRIELS DRAGON .... WHOLENESS

11°

MAGENTA DRAGON ....STRENGTH

12°

RAINBOW DRAGON ....MOVEMENT

13°

ORANGE DRAGON ....MOVEMENT

14°

GOLD CHRISTED DRAGON ....POSSESSIONS

15°

SILVER LUNA DRAGON ....PROTECTION

16°
BLUE DRAGON FROM THE PLEIADES ... JOURNEY

17°
BLACK DRAGON ... INITIATION

18°
GOLDEN ORANGE DRAGON ... DEFENCE

19°
DUSKY PINK DRAGON FROM ANDROMEDA...FLOW

20°
QUAN YINS PINK DRAGON ... BREAKTHROUGH

21 °
SOURCE DRAGON ... FLOW

22 °
GREEN GOLD DRAGON FROM SIRIUS ... SIGNALS

23°
EARTH AND WATER DRAGON ... WHOLENESS

24°
PURE WHITE DRAGON FROM ORION ... UNKNOWABLE

25°
EARTH DRAGON .... INITIATION

26°
BLACK DRAGON FROM SATURN ... GATEWAY

27°
GOLDEN ATLANTEAN DRAGON ... MOVEMENT

28°
THORS RED, BLACK AND GOLD DRAGON ... THE SELF

29°
FIRE AND WATER DRAGON ... STRENGTH

AQUARIUS

STAR SYSTEM: *CONSTELLATION OF AQUARIUS*
WORKING WITH OMEGA

FREQUENCY: 1185 HZ

This next Oracle represents The Rainbow Bridge which spans Aquarius into Pisces using Dragon and Crystal Energy. As a result, within this Oracle, you will find crystals that will help you along the way. Play with this frequency and contemplate the elements in the description and notice what comes in for you.

MEANING OF EACH DEGREE

0°
CRYSTAL YELLOW DRAGON ....GATEWAY

1°
AIR AND FIRE DRAGON ....STRENGTH

2°
GREEN DRAGON ....STANDSTILL

3°
ANGELIC DEGREE ... AIR ... MOLDAVITE ... PROTECTION

4°

AIR AIR WATER ... GRAPHIC SMOKEY QUARTZ ...
DISRUPTION

5°

AIR WATER ... CHRYSOCOLLA ... FLOW

6°

AIR WATER ... TRIGONIC QUARTZ ... STRENGTH

7°

AIR AIR FIRE ... PINK GRANITE... DISRUPTION

8°

AIR AIR FIRE ... APATITE ... CONSTRAINT

9°

AIR AIR FIRE ... LAVENDER ARAGONITE ... DEFENCE

10°

AIR AIR FIRE EARTH... CORNELIAN ... JOY

11°

AIR AIR EARTH ... HERKIMER DIAMOND... PROTECTION

12°

QUANTUM QUATTRO ....GROWTH

13°

EVOLUTIONARY DEGREE ... AIR AIR EARTH...
ANCESTRALITE ... INITIATION

14°

AIR AIR AIR ... ANANDALITE ... LUCKY /SOVRIEGNTY

15°

AIR AIR AIR ... BLOODSTONE ... OPENING

16°

AIR AIR AIR ... NIRVANA QUARTZ... GATEWAY

17°

AIR AIR WATER ... BLUE LACE AGATE ... DISRUPTION

18°

AIR AIR WATER ... ROSE QUARTZ ... WARRIOR

19°

AIR AIR WATER ... AURALITE ... UNKNOWABLE SPACE

20°

AIR AIR WATER /FIRE ... AMETHYST... MOVEMENT

21°

AIR AIR FIRE... MENALITE... UNKNOWABLE SPACE

22°

AIR AIR FIRE... SHIVALINGHAM... LUCKY SOVRIEGNTY

23°

AIR AIR FIRE... MOOKAITE JASPER ... JOY

24°

AIR AIR EARTH...AJOITE ...JOURNEY

25°

AIR AIR EARTH ... HALITE...GROWTH

26°

WISDOM DEGREE ... AIR AIR EARTH ... AZEZTULITE ...
SEPERATION

27°

AIR AIR AIR ....LAPISLAZULI............HARVEST

28°

AIR AIR AIR ... PRESELI BLUESTONE ...WARRIOR

29°

AIR AIR AIR ... EYE OF THE STORM ... PARTNERSHIP

PISCES

STAR SYSTEM: *CONSTELLATION OF PISCES*
WORKING WITH POLARIS

FREQUENCY: 432 HZ

MEANING OF EACH DEGREE

0°
AIR WATER ... BLACK TOURMALINE ... UNKNOWABLE
SPACE

1°
WATER WATER WATER ... RAINBOW MAYANITE ...
GATEWAY

2°
WATER WATER WATER ... TIGERS EYE... CONSTRAINT

3°
WATER, WATER, WATER ... GOLDEN HEALER ...
PROTECTION

4°
TRANSFORMATION............PARTNERSHIP

5°
PILLAR OF LIGHT ....HARVEST

6°
PRIESTESS............PARTNERSHIP

7°
MIRROR............CONSTRAINT

8°
THE CRUMBLING ....JOY

9°
AKASH ....INITIATION

10°
STAR SEED .... BREAKTHROUGH

11°
NO ....DEFENCE

12°
DON'T DIM TO FIT IN ....INITIATION

13°
SISTERHOOD OF THE ROSE ....FERTILITY

14°
COUNCIL OF THE LIGHT............STRENGTH

15°

SOUL FAMILY...........PROTECTION

16°

THE EVER UNFOLDING ROSE ....HARVEST

17°

ANNA, GRANDMOTHER OF JESUS...........DEFENCE

18°

THE AGE OF LIGHT ....FERTILITY

19°

TRUST YOUR PATH ....GATEWAY

20°

THE INITIATION ....SEPARATION

21°

GET GROUNDED .... BREAKTHROUGH

22°

UNBOUND............POSSESSIONS

23°

LEAP...........SIGNALS

24°

TRUST THE NIGGLE ....THE SELF

25°
INNER TEMPLE............PROTECTION

26 °
DANCE WITH LIFE ....DEFENCE

27°
DEEP REPLENISHMENT ....WARRIOR

28 °
AWAKENING ....WARRIOR

29 °
IMRAMA............DISRUPTION

00.00°
THE GREAT GATHERING THAT IS ARIES.

Chapter 7
The Key

So, let's put it all together.

1. Request a Natal Chart (which you can do for free on astro.com) and find a planet (e.g., Jupiter, Saturn)
2. Find which oracle the planet is in. For example, Sagittarius would be in the frequency of 963 **Hz.**
3. On the body map, locate where the planet is and which energy centre it belongs to. For example, Jupiter is the 'root'.
4. Then, find the corresponding affirmation by looking at which energy centre we are working with.

5. Jupiter means we know which energy centre or chakra), Jupiter rests in your root energy centre, which is the start place of expansion.

6. Then we look to the oracles, for example if Jupiter is on 18° and 22',within Sagittarius ,which is oracle 9. We then go to oracle 9, scroll down to 18, there you will find a 2 word meaning of this degree.

7. However there is an inner oracle, within Oracle 9, so we go to part 2 of Oracle 9 and find 18 again. Now we have 4 meanings to go with this frequency to help you to connect to what it means for you.

8. Now we have the energy centre (Root), we have the personal frequency (963 Hz), we have 4 definitions, and we have the affirmations of the root energy centre.

9. Simply put it all together.

Sit quietly.

Light a candle (if you wish to enable your mind to slow)

Play the frequency.

Say the affirmation 4 times.

Think of the two word meaning from the oracle

Think of the affirmation, how it registers with your journey ,your life, whatever you feel is right for you.

See what comes in for you...

Astrology does not limit you to your sun sign. You are all the oracles, just on this journey, your life, you have specific oracles to guide you, connect you, to assist you. Love, health, work challenges, you name it, it is endless, this is just the beginning.

Starting with ceres, your earth star energy, which helps you release physical, mental, and emotional pain with the frequency (vibration) of the collective, or your own Then work up.

Quick guide using frequency.

1. Do you feel any emotional, mental, or physical issues in your body?
2. Find the nearest energy centre, or a specific energy centre, depending on the issue.
3. The earth star is your natural pain killer.
4. Using the magnetics of the earth, bare feet will enable the release of any issue.

5. Ohm (136.1 hz) frequency great for inflammation.

6. Once you have found your frequency and you wish to release something out from your body, repeat 4x 4x day whilst playing or invoking the frequency *I RELEASE ALL RESISTANCE FROM* (say energy centre, part of the body or emotion)

7. If a physical issue, whilst playing or invoking the frequency after you have said the affirmation, cup your hands together and imagine white light growing within your cupped hands, then place this light on the area of the body and imagine the light going in to the area and spiralling in and around putting it back in to the perfect state. Do this as many times as you wish.

A Quick Guide to Energy Centres, Planets & Affirmations.

Each energy centre is associated with a planet. Here are the affirmations for those centres. To begin with, it is advised that you say 4x4x a day, start with playing the frequency, while saying the affirmation, to release the brain patterning, as well as instruct your field, all your body's, higher self, soul, and Universe, then relax and see what happens.

- Earth Star, Planet Ceres. Affirmation: I have a willingness to release.
- Left foot, Planet Venus and Right foot, Planet Mars. Affirmation: I have a willingness to balance.
- Root energy centre, Planet Jupiter. Affirmation: I have a willingness to expand.
- Sacral Energy Centre, The Sun (Our Star). Affirmation: I have a willingness to create
- Solar Plexus Energy Centre (left side), The Moon and Solar Plexus Energy Centre (right side), Planet Mercury. Affirmation: I Have a willingness to feel
- Heart Energy Centre (left side), Planet Neptune and Heart Energy Centre (right side), Planet Chiron. Affirmation: I love you (say your full name)/ I am love I love
- Throat Energy Centre, Planet Pluto. Affirmation: I have a willingness to change
- Third Eye Energy Centre (left side), Planet Uranus and Third Eye Energy Centre (right side), Planet Saturn. Affirmation: I have a willingness to se
- Crown Energy Centre, Asteroid Poseidon. Affirmation: I have a willingness to connect

Now that you have all the information, all you need to do is put it together.

Locate a planet ,which correlates to the the energy centre that will allow you to find the frequency you need.

You can find a frequency directory at dragonseyehub.com. You can also go to YouTube and put the frequency number you want to listen to or invoke ...

If you suffer from a physical ailment, find the energy centre closest to you, play or invoke the frequency, find the affirmation for that energy centre, then speak out loud or within, the affirmation with the frequency.

Look for what comes through for you. It may be through thought, instinct, picture, or emotion. It may be through synchronicity, what comes into your awareness physically, possibly through another person, a book, a TV program or movie, a song, or the internet.

The more you use it, the more your journey becomes self-evident.

USING IT MORE OFTEN MAKES IT VERY NATURAL, SO YOU CAN USE IT WITH ALL MODALITIES. THE TOOL CAN BE USED WHENEVER AND WHEREVER YOU LIKE. IT'S YOUR JOURNEY, YOUR TOOL. YOUR HOROSCOPE, YOUR BLUE PRINT IS MORE THAN YOU THINK IT IS. ONCE YOU FIND THE PLANET, WE KNOW ONE OF THE KEYS TO BEING AMAZING, THE NEW NORMAL.

WE FINISH THIS BOOK AS JUPITER FINISHES HIS 12-YEAR CYCLE.

* * *

Resources

- **dragonseyehub.com**
- YouTube; Dragonseyehub
- Facebook; Crystal nova
- Through these platforms, we continue to provide expanded information...
- Below are all the cards and runes used for the degree work, many thanks to their authors and artists. The authors and artists of these oracle decks are:
- The book of runes by Ralph.H. Blum
- The wild unknown Animal Spirit by Kim Krans
- The Keepers of the Light by Kyle Grey/Lily Moses
- The Star seed oracle by Rebecca Campbell /Danielle Noel

- Work your Light by Rebecca Campbell/Danielle Noel
- Dragon oracle by Diana Cooper /Carla Lee Morrow
- Moonology by Yasmin Bowland /Nyx Rowan
- Sacred Geometry Activations by LON
- The Secret Language of Color by Inna Legal
- The Crystal Healing Wisdom Oracle by Judy Hall /Michael Illas
- The Good Tarot by Colette Baron-Reid /Jenna DellaGrottaglia
- Oracle of the 7 by Colette Baron-Reid/Jenna DellaGrottaglia
- Titania´s (madame Len Ormand's) Fortune Cards by Tatiana Hardie
- Sacred Geometry Healing Cards by Emily Kasarda /Kenz

Acknowledgments

Lastly, I would like to thank all our friends and family, soul family, Council of Three, Father Mother and All that is (FMA) Sam, Riv, Bing, Axel, and Lilith, who we have worked with, laughed with, and helped us throughout this life and all lives .

Sam

Riv

Bing

AMM

Axel

Lilith

Council of Three

F,M,A

The Council of the Three

The Black Box from Upsilom within the Andromeda

To facilitate this work, I am the man on the ground, while they are the team in other dimensions, star systems, and

Universes who are encouraging our conscious growth, our conscious evolution.

About the Author

My name is Pennie, I'm an astrologer and channeler, I have been guided to open the Dragons Eye school of empowerment here in the south of france in a beautiful place surrounded by amazing energy and mountains. Where we can share and empower one another.

For more information, please visit
dragonseyehub.com

Printed in Great Britain
by Amazon